N. T. WRIGHT
FOR EVERYONE
BIBLE STUDY GUIDES

LUKE

26 STUDIES FOR INDIVIDUALS OR GROUPS

N. T. WRIGHT

WITH PATTY PELL

IVP Connect

An imprint of InterVarsity Press
Downers Grove, Illinois

InterVarsity Press
P.O. Box 1400, Downers Grove, IL 60515-1426
World Wide Web: www.ivpress.com
E-mail: email@ivpress.com

This study guide is based on and includes excerpts adapted from Luke for Everyone, *© 2001, 2004 Nicholas Thomas Wright. All Scripture quotations, unless otherwise indicated, are taken from the New Testament for Everyone. Copyright © 2001-2008 by Nicholas Thomas Wright. Used by permission of SPCK, London. All rights reserved.*

InterVarsity Press® is the book-publishing division of InterVarsity Christian Fellowship/USA®, a movement of students and faculty active on campus at hundreds of universities, colleges and schools of nursing in the United States of America, and a member movement of the International Fellowship of Evangelical Students. For information about local and regional activities, write Public Relations Dept., InterVarsity Christian Fellowship/USA, 6400 Schroeder Rd., P.O. Box 7895, Madison, WI 53707-7895, or visit the IVCF website at <www.intervarsity.org>.

Design: Cindy Kiple
Cover image: Jupiterimages

ISBN 978-0-8308-2183-9

Printed in the United States of America ∞

P	18	17	16	15	14	13	12	11	10	9	8	7	6
Y	26	25	24	23	22	21	20	19	18	17			

CONTENTS

GETTING THE MOST
OUT OF LUKE

Imagine a village in ancient Palestine. They didn't have printed books or newspapers, television or radio. They had official storytellers. Some great event would happen: an earthquake, a battle or the visit of an emperor. Within a day or two the story would be told all round the village, and would settle into a regular form. Everyone would know the story, but some of the better storytellers in the village would be recognized by the others as the right people to tell it.

And that's what they'd do. They wouldn't change the story or modify it; if they did, people would notice and set them straight. So when Luke went round the villages of Palestine and Syria in the second half of the first century, listening to the stories told by the accredited storytellers—"the stewards of the word," as he calls them—he would know he was in touch with solid, reliable evidence that went right back to the early events. Plato had said, five hundred years earlier, that there was a danger in writing things down; human memories, he thought, were the best way to get things right and pass them on. In the century after Luke, one of the great Christian teachers declared that he preferred living testimony to writings. You can't tell where a book has come from, but you can look witnesses in the eye, and use your judgment about whether to trust them.

So, why is Luke writing it all down now? And who was Luke anyway? We actually don't know for certain who the author of this book was, but we call him "Luke" because that's who the church, from very early on, said had written this Gospel and the Acts of the Apostles too. He may well have been the Luke whom Paul mentions as his companion (Colossians 4:14; Philemon 24; 2 Timothy 4:11). He could have been writing any time between A.D. 50 and 90. A fair guess is that the author is Luke, one of Paul's companions, and that he was writing in the 60s or 70s. Why write such a book now?

The main reason is that the message about Jesus has spread far and wide, way beyond the original communities in the regions Jesus himself visited. Peter, Paul and other missionaries had carried the message in all directions, and doubtless there were garbled, muddled and misleading reports circulating about who exactly Jesus was, what he did and said, and what had happened to him. Luke knows of other writings that have begun the task of putting it down on paper, but he has a wider audience in mind, an educated, intelligent, enquiring public.

A further reason, if indeed Luke is writing in the late 60s and 70s, would be the horrendous war that was raging in Palestine at the time. The Jews rebelled against the occupying Roman forces in 66, until finally, after a long siege, Jerusalem was destroyed in 70. The result was that many towns and villages where Jesus had been seen and known were decimated. Not only was the older generation dying out, but communities that had witnessed Jesus' activities were being dispersed or destroyed. The stories, which depended for transmission on a peaceful, stable society, were in danger of dying out. Unless steps were taken to write them down, the message would not be passed on to the next generation. And since Luke, like all the early Christians, believed that the things that had actually happened (what we would call the historical facts) had changed the course of the world, it was vital that they be presented as clearly and unambiguously as possible.

Luke thus constructs a grand doorway into his Gospel. He invites us to come in and make ourselves at home. Here we will find security, a solid basis for lasting faith.

SUGGESTIONS FOR INDIVIDUAL STUDY

1. As you begin each study, pray that God will speak to you through his Word.

2. Read the introduction to the study and respond to the "Open" question that follows it. This is designed to help you get into the theme of the study.

3. Read and reread the Bible passage to be studied. Each study is designed to help you consider the meaning of the passage in its context. The commentary and questions in this guide are based on my own translation of each passage found in the companion volume to this guide in the For Everyone series on the New Testament (published by SPCK and Westminster John Knox).

4. Write your answers to the questions in the spaces provided or in a personal journal. Each study includes three types of questions: observation questions, which ask about the basic facts in the passage; interpretation questions, which delve into the meaning of the passage; and application questions, which help you discover the implications of the text for growing in Christ. Writing out your responses can bring clarity and deeper understanding of yourself and of God's Word.

5. Each session features selected comments from the For Everyone series. These notes provide further biblical and cultural background and contextual information. They are designed not to answer the questions for you but to help you along as you study the Bible for yourself. For even more reflections on each passage, you may wish to have on hand a copy of the companion volume from the For Everyone series as you work through this study guide.

6. Use the guidelines in the "Pray" section to focus on God, thanking him for what you have learned and praying about the applications that have come to mind.

SUGGESTIONS FOR GROUP MEMBERS

1. Come to the study prepared. Follow the suggestions for individual study mentioned above. You will find that careful preparation will greatly enrich your time spent in group discussion.

2. Be willing to participate in the discussion. The leader of your group will not be lecturing. Instead, she or he will be asking the questions found in this guide and encouraging the members of the group to discuss what they have learned.

3. Stick to the topic being discussed. These studies focus on a particular passage of Scripture. Only rarely should you refer to other portions of the Bible or outside sources. This allows for everyone to participate on equal ground and for in-depth study.

4. Be sensitive to the other members of the group. Listen attentively when they describe what they have learned. You may be surprised by their insights! Each question assumes a variety of answers. Many questions do not have "right" answers, particularly questions that aim at meaning or application. Instead the questions push us to explore the passage more thoroughly.

   When possible, link what you say to the comments of others. Also, be affirming whenever you can. This will encourage some of the more hesitant members of the group to participate.

5. Be careful not to dominate the discussion. We are sometimes so eager to express our thoughts that we leave too little opportunity for others to respond. By all means participate! But allow others to also.

6. Expect God to teach you through the passage being discussed and through the other members of the group. Pray that you will have an enjoyable and profitable time together, but also that as a result of the study you will find ways that you can take action individually and/ or as a group.

7. It will be helpful for groups to follow a few basic guidelines. These guidelines, which you may wish to adapt to your situation, should be read at the beginning of the first session.

   • Anything said in the group is considered confidential and will not be discussed outside the group unless specific permission is given to do so.

- We will provide time for each person present to talk if he or she feels comfortable doing so.

- We will talk about ourselves and our own situations, avoiding conversation about other people.

- We will listen attentively to each other.

- We will be very cautious about giving advice.

Additional suggestions for the group leader can be found at the back of the guide.

1

ANNOUNCING
THE BIRTHS

Luke 1:1-38

One of the most visited exhibits in the famous Irish city of Dublin is the Book of Kells, the center of a special display in Trinity College. This wonderfully ornamented manuscript of the Gospels dates to around A.D. 800—considerably closer in time to the New Testament than to us today.

The people who arranged the exhibition don't let the public see the Gospels themselves straight away. Wisely, they lead you first past several other very old books, which prepare you step by step for the great treasure itself. By the time you reach the heart of the exhibition you have already thought your way back to the world of early Celtic Christianity, to the monks who spent years of their life painstakingly copying out parts of the Bible and lavishly decorating it. You are now ready to appreciate it properly.

Luke has done something similar in the opening of his Gospel. His story is of course principally about Jesus, but the name *Jesus* doesn't occur for the first thirty verses. Luke knows we will need to prepare our minds and hearts for this story. So he begins with the story of a devout couple going about their daily lives.

OPEN

Describe a time when someone asked you to do something that would be difficult or scary, but that you knew would also be good. What was your initial reaction to the request?

STUDY

1. *Read Luke 1:1-38.* Verses 1-4 form a prologue to the Gospel of Luke. What does the prologue tell us about Luke's purposes and methods?

2. We read of Gabriel's visit to Zechariah in verses 5-25. Describe Zechariah and Elizabeth. Who are they, and what is their life like before the angel visits? Simple, respected.

3. The couple, well past childbearing age, are going to have a son at last, in a culture where childless women were mocked. The story would have reminded Jews of that day of Abraham and Sarah having a child in their old age (Genesis 21), Rachel bearing Jacob two sons after years of childlessness (Genesis 30 and 35), and particularly the births of Samson (Judges 13) and Samuel (1 Samuel 1).

    What is Luke seeking to emphasize through the details he chooses to tell of Zechariah and Elizabeth's story?
    5- Worthy, 6-Obedient/righteous, 7-grown old
    & childless

4. Like all priests except the chief priests, who lived in Jerusalem itself, Zechariah would come in to the city when it was the turn of his division to perform the regular temple liturgy; he would stay in lodgings within the temple precincts, and then return home to continue his normal work as a teacher and leader in the local community.

   Abijah, hill country of Judah V.39

   How does Zechariah show a mixture of half-faith and devotion in his encounter with Gabriel? *How can I be sure of this = Prove it.*

5. Luke is careful not to dress up the story by making Zechariah a great hero of faith. Here we have an ordinary husband and wife receiving an extraordinary message from the angel and responding in mixed ways. What does this tell us about how God works?

   Using people just like us.

6. How does the story of Zechariah and Elizabeth prepare us for the story of the conception and birth of Jesus? *Miracle, level 1*

Mary's story in verses 26-38 is told both by Luke and Matthew, in versions so different that they can hardly be dependent on one another; in other words, the story seems to have been widely known in the very early church, rather than being a fantasy invented several generations after the fact. People of Luke's day knew just as well as we do where babies come from, and Luke knew the reaction people would have to this story. There would be little reason for Luke and Matthew to pass on such a story unless they had good reason to suppose it was true.

7. In what ways are the stories of Zechariah and Mary similar and different? *Prove it* "How can I
    Humble confusion, personal so
    perhaps deserves explanation

8. What is the political or royal meaning that Luke gives the event in verses 26-38? *Throne of David, over the house*
    of Jacob, unending

    In addition to Jesus being born a descendant of King David, a descendant who will be a king like David, other political references are made (verses 32-33). This coming king would be, in some sense, "God's son" (see Psalm 89:27). As with a good deal of New Testament language about Jesus, this is both a theological claim and a huge political claim. It was theological in that Jesus is somehow identified with God in a unique way which people then and now find hard to grasp and believe. And it was political because "son of God" was a title commonly applied to Caesar in that day. So what is being said here is that Jesus is the true ruler of the world, not Caesar, and certainly not the powers of the world today.

9. What are the implications of the Holy Spirit coming upon Mary and the power of the Most High God overshadowing her?
    Invasion

10. Put all this together—the conception of a baby, the power of God, and the challenge to all human empires—and we can see why the story is so explosive. Perhaps some of the controversy about whether Mary could have conceived Jesus without a human father is because, deep down, we don't want to think that there might be a king who could claim this sort of origin and therefore this sort of absolute allegiance. How do people respond to a notion that there is one who deserves our absolute allegiance? *reject -*

11. Think of something God has called you to—a task or a role, perhaps—in the last five years. How did you respond—more like Zechariah or more like Mary? *teaching as needed.*

12. In the midst of the fulfillment of God's promises and purposes for the whole world, he also considers the needs, hopes and fears of ordinary people like Zechariah, Elizabeth and Mary. How do you respond to this as you consider your own needs, hopes and fears? *Don't think about life in this way.*

PRAY

Begin with prayers of praise that God fulfills his purposes through ordinary people in the midst of their ordinary lives. Then, spend some time praying for the courage to respond to God's call like Mary with humility and acceptance.

2

SONGS OF PRAISE

Luke 1:39-80

Many people today can't imagine what life would be like without a television. We are so used to it telling us what to think about all the time that, without it, some people become quite worried, lost in a world of their own unfamiliar thoughts like an explorer whose guide has just disappeared. Take away radio, the Internet and newspapers as well, and . . . what would *you* think about all day?

That was the situation, of course, of most people in the world until very recently. It was the situation for everybody in Jesus' time. If you were Zechariah, what would you think of all day? Your family, certainly. Local village business, presumably. Your health, quite possibly. The state of the crops, the prospect for harvest.

But behind these obvious concerns, there are deeper questions. Something is wrong in the world. People are suffering. *Your* people are suffering. Wicked foreigners have come from far away, with hatred in their eyes and weapons in their hands. Death and darkness have stalked the land. Many people in many countries have had all this to think about over many centuries.

Behind that again, there may be a sense that, though much has gone wrong, somehow there is a larger hope. In the remaining verses of chapter 1, Luke displays both of these perspectives through ordinary characters in God's story.

OPEN

What would make you celebrate wildly, without inhibition, right now?

STUDY

1. *Read Luke 1:39-56.* Two cousins, an old woman and an unmarried young woman, meet for the first time after each has become pregnant. In such a setting, what emotions would you expect to spring up between them?

2. What is surprising about the way Mary and Elizabeth actually respond to each other, given their situations?

3. In verses 39-56 we find Mary's song of celebration (often called *Magnificat* because that is the first word of the poem in Latin). It is one of the most famous songs in Christianity. What causes Mary to launch into a song like this?

4. What characteristics of God does Mary's song highlight?

5. Almost every word of Mary's song is a biblical quotation. Much of it echoes the song of Hannah in 1 Samuel 2. For centuries Israel had held on to God's promises to Abraham that all nations would be blessed through his family, that the powers that kept the world in slavery would be toppled, that the poor and hungry would be lifted up. God would win a victory over the greedy, the power-hungry, the forces of evil. Mary and Elizabeth knew all too well about this personally, living as they did in the dark days of Herod the Great, whose casual brutality was backed up with Roman might.

   What are the wrongs to be righted, the changes in society that you long for which may seem too massive and difficult to do anything about?

6. In what ways, even small ones, can you be involved in this work that God desires in his world?

7. What sections of Mary's song resonate with your own heart and life right now, and provide hope or encouragement?

8. *Read Luke 1:57-80.* What do we learn about the person of Zechariah from this section?

9. How does Zechariah's song weave together the political and the spiritual?

10. What similarities and differences do you see between Mary's song and Zechariah's?

Zechariah's own story of nine months' silence suddenly broken at the naming of the child is a reflection on a smaller scale of what was going on in the Israel of his day. Prophecy, many believed, had been silent for a long time. Now it was going to burst out again, to lead many back to a true allegiance to their God. What had begun as a kind of punishment for Zechariah's lack of faith now turns into a new sort of sign, a sign that God is doing a new thing.

11. Luke's first chapter holds together what we often find easier to keep separate. How does this first chapter display a concern for both the larger perspective of God's purpose in history and the lives of ordinary people?

12. How do you see God's larger purposes in the world intersecting with your own life, your individual hopes, dreams and fears?

PRAY

Using Mary's Magnificat as a guide, give praise to God using the very words of Scripture to inform your prayers. Interject your personal prayers of praise. Pray also for the major problems of oppression, hunger, greed and violence around the world.

3

THE BIRTH OF JESUS

Luke 2

If you try to point out something to a dog, the dog will often look at your finger instead of at the object you're trying to point to. This is frustrating, but it illustrates a natural mistake we all make from time to time. It's the mistake many people make when reading the Christmas story in Luke's Gospel: focusing on the manger—the Christmas crib. The most famous animal feeding-trough in all history. To concentrate on the manger and to forget why it was mentioned in the first place is like the dog looking at the finger rather than the object.

The point Luke is making is clear. The birth of this little boy is the beginning of a confrontation between the kingdom of God and the kingdoms of the world. Augustus never heard of Jesus of Nazareth. But within a century or so his successors in Rome had not only heard of him; they were taking steps to obliterate his followers. Just over three centuries later, a Roman emperor became a Christian.

Luke's narrative reminds us not to stop at the manger but to see the explosive truth it's pointing to.

OPEN

What is your favorite Christmas carol and why? I Heard the Bells

STUDY

1. *Read Luke 2:1-20.* Though the feeding-trough itself is not the point, Luke mentions it three times in these verses. What practical function does it serve in the drama of Luke's story in these verses?

   Unique marker =sign

2. How do you think you would have reacted if you experienced what the shepherds did?

   Similar

3. Luke introduces the story of Jesus' birth by telling his readers about Augustus Caesar, way off in Rome, at the height of his power. Augustus was the adopted son of Julius Caesar. He became sole ruler of the Roman world after a bloody civil war in which he overpowered all rival claimants. The last to be destroyed was the famous Mark Antony, who committed suicide not long after his defeat at the battle of Actium in 31 B.C.

   Augustus turned the great Roman republic into an empire, with himself as the head; he proclaimed that he had brought justice and peace to the whole world and, declaring his dead adoptive father to be divine, styled himself as "son of god." Poets wrote songs about the new era that had begun; historians told the long story of Rome's rise to greatness, reaching its climax with Augustus himself. Augustus, people said, was the "savior" of the world. He was its king, its "lord." Increasingly, in the eastern part of his empire, people worshiped him, too, as a god.

   What similarities and contrasts is Luke setting up in verses 1-20 between Jesus and Augustus Caesar?

   Son of God   son of god Julius

4. At Christmas our focus is often on gift-giving, big meals, music concerts, family gatherings and, yes, a story of a newborn baby. What are the things Luke is emphasizing in his story?

   Angels proclaim from God (so we need to listen)
   Shepherds seek to confirm (so we need to refresh our minds)
   Spread the Word (we need to share)
   Mary pondered (we need to mediate quietly)

5. *Read Luke 2:21-52.* What do we learn about Mary and Joseph in verses 21-23? *Observant, obedient of the Law and God's instruction*

6. Another man and woman are also in the temple—Simeon and Anna. Simeon is waiting for God to comfort Israel. Anna is in touch with the people who are waiting for the redemption of Israel. They are both living in a world of patient hope, where suffering has become a way of life.

   What does Simeon mean by referring to Jesus as a light for revelation to the nations, and glory for God's people Israel in verse 32? *Israel has the honor of fulfilling God's mission to the world*

7. And what does he mean by saying that this child will make many in Israel fall and rise again, and be a sign spoken against so that many hearts will be disclosed (vv. 34-35)? *Think entrenched power & order — Pharisees, etc.*

8. What might Joseph and Mary be feeling after hearing both Simeon's and Anna's words? *Affirmed in their visions*

9. How is Mary's reaction in verse 48 at finding Jesus in the temple so understandable?

   Parental protection. Focused on the everyday without time to see the "big picture"

10. What does Jesus realize about his purposes that Mary does not understand?

11. This is not the first or last time in this Gospel that Jesus will surprise those he is with—or us. He doesn't do or say what is expected. Every time we relax and think we've really understood him and where he's going, he will be up ahead, or perhaps stay behind while we go on without thinking.

    How have you found that following Jesus involves the unexpected?

12. By the time the first two chapters of Luke are finished, almost all his readers will have found someone in the story with whom they can iden-

tify. We have met the older couple surprised to be having a child. We have seen the young girl even more surprised to have a child so soon, and her husband coming with her to the temple to offer the specified sacrifice. There are shepherds out with their sheep at night receiving a startling message and going to see if it's true. Then an old man and woman, waiting their turn to die and praying for the salvation of God's people. Then we see young parents anxious about a "lost" son.

With whom do you identify in the first two chapters, and why?

PRAY

Spend time praying to be faithful in responding to God's work in your life. Pray that he would use you—whatever age and stage you're at, with your unique gifts and personalities—to help bring his countercultural kingdom to earth, and pray for courage to be obedient to his leading.

JOHN THE BAPTIST

Luke 3

Behind the events of chapter 3 of Luke's Gospel is a story of oppression and misery that was building up to an explosion. Rome had ruled the area for about a hundred years, but only since A.D. 6 had there been a Roman governor resident in the area, living in Caesarea (on the Mediterranean coast) but also keeping a base in Jerusalem. Augustus Caesar, the first emperor, had died in A.D. 14, and his place had been taken by the ruthless Tiberius, who was already being worshiped as a god in the eastern parts of the empire.

Two sons of Herod the Great, Herod Antipas and Philip, were ruling somewhat shakily under Roman permission, in the north of the country, but Rome had taken direct control of the south, including Jerusalem itself. Most Jews did not regard Herod's sons as real rulers; they were a self-made royal house, ruling, like Rome, by fear and oppression. The high priests weren't much better. Popular movements of resistance had come and gone, in some cases being brutally put down.

Everybody knew they couldn't go on as they were. Something had to happen. But what?

OPEN

Talk about your family history. How far back can you trace your family?

From where did your ancestors originate? Do you know a story about a distant ancestor?

STUDY

1. *Read Luke 3:1-20.* What is Luke's introduction to the story in 3:1-2 designed to do for the reader? Document historical fact. Describes oppressive rule

2. When there is an crisis such as a flood, authorities give warning to the people. Imminent danger needs urgent action. What was the emergency that John was declaring in verses 3-9?
    "coming wrath" (v.7)

3. In what ways is John living out the quote that he uses from the book of Isaiah in 3:4-6? Calling for repentance

4. How is John using the image of a tree in verses 7-9 to confront the crowds about their own lives? Unhealthy tree is cut down

5. Baptism, plunging into the river Jordan, was a powerful sign of renewal. When the children of Israel had come out of slavery in Egypt—a story they all knew well because of their regular Passovers and other festivals—they were brought through the Red Sea, through the Sinai wilderness, then through the Jordan into the Promised Land. Now they were in slavery again (this time to Rome), and wanted a new exodus to bring them to freedom. They believed their current sorry state was due to Israel's sin. So John calls them to repent and to once more go into and out of the Jordan to signify their return to God with heart and soul.

   What are the common themes in John's answer to the people's questions in 3:10-14? *Justice & mercy commanded.*

6. What do we learn about tax collectors and soldiers in John's time from the instructions he gives them? *Part of Oppression*

7. If John were to come down the main street of your town with a megaphone, what would he be saying?

8. Herod Antipas, officially a tetrarch—a kind of second-rank prince— had had an affair with Herodias, the wife of his brother Philip, after which she had divorced Philip and married Antipas. John's denunciation of this flagrant and incestuous adultery was not simply a moral criticism. If Herod had any pretensions to being the true king

of the Jews, behavior like that would prove him a fraud.

Herod, you see, had been working on rebuilding the temple, which was itself a way of claiming royal status. King Solomon had been the first temple-builder, and some of Israel's greatest kings had rebuilt or restored the temple. Herod was hoping to inherit his father's title, king of the Jews. But John had other ideas about the true King of the Jews.

In verses 16-20, how is the Messiah, the king of the Jews, presented as both a judge and savior? *changed by HS.*
refined with fire

9. In what ways throughout this chapter does Luke's vision of God's kingdom differ from the kingdom of Herod?

10. *Read Luke 3:21-38.* The heavenly voice in verse 22 echoes the words of God to Abraham (Genesis 22:2) and of Isaiah the prophet (42:1), commissioning the Messiah as the Servant, the one who will suffer and die for the people and the world. How is the voice during the baptism of Jesus both a wonderful affirmation and a clear reminder of the path ahead for Jesus? *My son whom I love*

11. What names do you recognize in the genealogy of Jesus in verses 23-38, and what do you know about them? *David -great king, Jesse, Obed, Boaz, Judah, Jacob, Isaac, Abraham, Shem, Noah, Lamech, Methuselah, Seth, Adam, God.*

The one link between the family tree and what goes before and comes after is the final phrase: Jesus is the son of God. Of course, by that reckoning so is everyone else in the list, from Joseph right back to Adam. Luke certainly means more than this when he uses the phrase "son of God" as a title for Jesus (1:35; 3:22; 4:3 and 9). Perhaps it is best to see the family tree stretching back to the creation of the world, as a way of saying that, though Jesus is indeed the Messiah of Israel (another meaning of "son of God"), he is so precisely for the whole world. All creation, the whole human race, will benefit from what he has come to do.

12. How has the quiet voice of the Holy Spirit reminded you of God's affirming love while also calling you forward to what lies ahead?

Believe "You say I am loved, when I can't feel a thing"

PRAY

Begin with prayers of confession for the ways and times you haven't produced good fruit in recent weeks. Then, move to prayers of thanksgiving for the affirming voice of the Holy Spirit as he pours out his love on us and calls us into the work of the kingdom.

NOTE ON LUKE 3:23-38

Matthew and Luke give two different family trees for Jesus. Ever since the early days of the church, learned scholars have struggled to give good answers as to why, and most have admitted defeat.

In a small and close-knit community, there is every probability that someone could trace their descent from the same source by two or more different routes, depending on how much intermarrying had taken place. After my own parents were married, they discovered that they were distant cousins with one remove of generation. In the little country of Israel between the time of David and Jesus, similar things could easily have happened. Many could have traced their descent to the same ancestors by at least two routes.

Luke, it seems, wants to declare that Jesus was not only a true Jew but a descendant of David and Zerubbabel—part of a genuinely royal family. He was counted as Joseph's adopted son, which served, it seems, for this purpose of securing his kingly heritage.

JESUS' MINISTRY BEGINS

Luke 4

Jesus was not Superman. Many today, including some devout Christians, see him as a kind of Christian version of the movie character, able to do whatever he wanted, to "zap" reality into any shape he liked. In the movies, Superman looks like an ordinary human being, but really he isn't. Underneath the disguise he is all-powerful, a kind of computer-age super-magician. That's not the picture of Jesus we get in the New Testament.

Luke has just reminded us of Jesus' membership in the family of Adam. If there had been any doubt about his being really human, Luke underlines his sharing of our flesh and blood in this vivid scene of temptation. If Jesus is the descendant of Adam, he must now face not only what Adam faced but the powers that had been unleashed through human rebellion and sin. Long years of habitual rebellion against the creator God had brought about a situation in which the world, the flesh and the devil had become used to twisting human beings into whatever shape they wanted.

OPEN

Think about a time when God was calling you to a new phase of life or ministry. What roadblocks or temptations did you face?

STUDY

1. *Read Luke 4:1-30.* What echoes of the story of Adam and Eve are seen in the temptation story in 4:1-13?

    Bodily needs
    Thirst for power/recognition (praise from men)
    Expectation of protection from
    world (gravity)

2. What is the nature of each temptation that Jesus faces from Satan?

    Food
    Pleasing to eye
    gaining wisdom

3. In Israel there had been other royal movements in Jesus' time, not only the well-known house of Herod but also other lesser-known figures such as Athronges who gathered followers and were hailed as kings, only to be cut down by Roman or Herodian troops. There were would-be prophets who promised their followers signs from heaven and great miracles to show God's saving power. They did not last long.

    In contrast to these figures, how do the three temptations show what kind of messiahship Jesus was to pursue?

    Dependence on Holy Spirit and subordinate
    to God.

4. What is significant about the way in which Jesus defeated Satan in this temptation story?

    Scripture I need to think "what
    script" applies?

5. We are unlikely to be tempted in exactly the same way as Jesus was,
   but every Christian will be tested at the points which matter most
   in his or her life and vocation. How can we learn to recognize and
   defeat the voices that whisper attractive lies to us?

6. How do Jesus' listeners initially react (Luke 4:22) when he begins
   his public ministry by quoting from Isaiah 61:1-2?

   *Spoke well when they thought
   his positive words were for them.
   Proud of the hometown celeb.*

7. Jesus deliberately stops short his quotation from Isaiah. He leaves out
   the words in Isaiah 61:3 about proclaiming "the day of vengeance of
   our God." Then in 4:25-27 he points out that the great prophet Elijah
   was sent to help a widow—but not a Jewish one. And another great
   prophet Elisha healed one solitary leper—who was the commander
   of the enemy army.

   Why did all this make the crowds so upset that they kick Jesus out of
   the synagogue and hustle him out of town with the intent of throwing him down from the edge of a cliff?

   *Messiah is for Israel alone.
   made furious*

8. How is the idea of grace for all people, even those we disagree with
   or fight against, a challenge to our interests and agendas today?

9. *Read Luke 4:31-44.* What astonished people about Jesus?

10. Why was Jesus committed to spending most of his time on the move rather than staying in one place?

11. How do verses 31-44 offer a taste of Jesus fulfilling the passage in Isaiah that he quotes in Nazareth?

    Cast out evil spirits; Simon's mother-in-law, multiple healings, more evil spirits

12. In what areas of either your personal life or the world around you do you long to see this passage fulfilled by Jesus?

PRAY

Thank Jesus for the ways in which he has brought the Isaiah passage to fulfillment. Then intercede for others who have not seen the same kind of healing, release or redemption.

6

MIRACLES, HEALINGS AND PARTIES

Luke 5

We live in an age where everything new will soon be old. Whether it is the latest computer or television or style of music or medication, we know that the process of research and development is going on and on. And with that is an army of people who want to let you know about everything that's new in hopes that you will buy.

But in the world of Jesus and his followers, novelty was deeply threatening, especially when people had built their lives around the old way. Don't expect people who have given years to the old ways to be happy about switching allegiance. They want to stay with what they know. Think how those who provided horses or stagecoaches for travel reacted when trains and then cars arrived. Jesus claims to be bringing a new kingdom-program on the scene, and in Luke 5 we find a variety of ways in which he gives evidence of that. But not everyone is happy with what they see.

OPEN

When were you unhappy for something new to arrive or be offered that threatened to displace the old thing or way you were comfortable with?

STUDY

1. *Read Luke 5:1-16.* Along the lakeshore close to Capernaum there is a sequence of steep inlets, a zigzagging shoreline with each inlet forming a natural amphitheater. To this day, if you get in a boat and push out a little from the shore, you can talk in quite a natural voice, and anyone on the slopes of the inlet can hear you clearly—more clearly, in fact, than if you were right there on the shore with them.

   Now put yourself in the place of Peter in this story. Think about what you normally do day after day, and then imagine Jesus suddenly appearing and asking for your help, and then asking you to do something in your own area of expertise. What might be going through your mind during the events described in 5:1-4?

2. Why does the huge catch of fish cause Peter to react the way he does in verses 5-11?

3. Most of the ancient Jewish purity laws were the equivalent of what today we think of as normal hygienic practice. They were intended to prevent the spread of disease. This explains why Jesus (here and in Luke 17:12-19) told sufferers to go show themselves to the priests. If someone wanted a clean bill of health, it was the priest's job to examine the person and declare if the person was clean. If so, then he or she could rejoin his family and his community as a full and accepted member.

   What is so significant about how Jesus heals the leper?

4. What do we learn about Jesus' priorities as we read 5:15-16?

5. In light of this, how would you assess your own schedule and the demands on your time?

6. *Read 5:17-39.* The Pharisees were a pressure group, not an official body. This is the first time Luke has introduced us to them, and here we see this influential organization is in force, from all over the small country. The Pharisees' agenda was to intensify observance of the Jewish law. That, they believed, would create the conditions for God to act, as he had promised, to judge the pagans who were oppressing Israel and to liberate his people.

   Why would the Pharisees gather like this to check out this young prophet?

7. After the friends lowered the paralyzed man through the roof, why were the Pharisees so troubled and upset at Jesus?

8. Upon seeing the faith of the friends, Jesus forgave and then healed the paralyzed man. How does Jesus connect faith and the power of God?

9. Who are the characters and what are the points of tension present in the episode found in 5:27-39?

10. In what ways are verses 31-32 a "mission statement" for Jesus?

11. Luke 5:34 describes a party—the first of many in Luke's Gospel— and like all Jesus' parties it is a sign of the new age. It is, for those with eyes to see, a miniature messianic banquet. Luke then attaches to this story a string of short sayings in 5:36-39. How do these sayings reflect how new his kingdom message actually is?

12. The challenge of this passage and the whole fifth chapter is to see where people are living as though the old age was still the norm, as though the new life of the gospel had never burst in upon us.

    Where in your life do you still live as if the old age was in effect?

13. Looking back over the events in Luke 5, what would it look like for you to live in the promise of the new kingdom?

PRAY

Sit in silence for a few moments and ask the Lord to touch the areas of your life that you identified in question 5. Pray for the new kingdom and the power of Jesus to reign in that place. Then, spend a few moments praying in response to your answers to questions 12 and 13.

NOTE ON LUKE 5:24

Jesus explains what he is doing by the mysterious phrase "the son of man." In Daniel 7 "one like a son of man" is brought before God, after a time of great persecution, and is given authority over the world. The phrase could simply mean "a human being," but the way Daniel 7 was read by many Jews in Jesus' day gave the figure a much more specific meaning. This would be the Messiah, the one through whom God would set up his kingdom at last after Israel's long suffering.

Perhaps not all of Jesus' hearers would have understood that, but many would see that he was making a huge claim to authority. His actions and words were God's real kingdom work. At a stroke, Jesus has summoned up a lively element from the Jewish thought of the time and pressed it into service in his own cause. The healing of the paralyzed man functions as he intended it to, as a sign that this authority was real.

7

TRUE OBEDIENCE

Luke 6

How must Jesus have appeared to many onlookers? He held no public office. He was not a priest. He wasn't part of any well-known pressure groups, such as the Pharisees, who had their own opinions on how the law should be kept, which they tried to insist on for society as a whole. He hadn't had any formal training as a teacher.

And yet there he was telling people what to do, giving people permission to do things they were not normally supposed to do. Who did he think he was? That is, in fact, the main question Luke wants us to ask. Luke is not so interested in asking, "Do we or don't we keep the sabbath?" but rather, "Who did Jesus think he was?"

OPEN

How do people today try to enlist Jesus to support their own groups or causes?

STUDY

1. *Read Luke 6:1-26.* In verses 1-5, Jesus refers to David, some thousand years before, who was leading a rag-tag group of followers, keeping away from King Saul, waiting for the time when David's kingship would arrive. David's men were hungry, so they ate the "bread of the Presence" (the bread which was set aside to symbolize God's presence in fellowship with his people). Normally only priests in the sanctuary were allowed to eat the bread, but David claimed he (and his followers) had the right to do so.

   1 Sam 21:3-6

   What is Jesus suggesting by telling this story about David and his followers?

   Sabbath is for people, not people for the Sabbath.

2. For many Christians in today's world, keeping the sabbath has become a quaint memory. But for Jesus' contemporaries, the sabbath was one of the chief badges of their identity in a hostile world, a sign to them and their neighbors that they were God's special people. It's easy for modern Western Christians to mock the Jews of Jesus' day for fussing about something that doesn't concern us. Yet there are many things in our society which have become just as central for us—and perhaps just as much under God's judgment—as sabbath-keeping was for them.

   What practices, traditions or rules do we tend to cling to today in the way the Jews of Jesus' time clung to their sabbath-keeping?

3. Every Jew knew that Israel originally had twelve tribes. In 6:12-16, then, what was Jesus implying by choosing twelve disciples to be with him and do ministry with him?

   The "new Israel 'people of God'"

4. The four promises and four warnings of verses 17-26 are presented in terms of Israel's great scriptural codes of blessings and curses from the book of Deuteronomy (such as chapters 27–28). These formed part of the covenant (a charter or binding agreement) between God and Israel.

   In what ways are these promises and warnings an upside-down covenant?

5. What do Jesus' promises and warnings for our world today look like for people who will hear his call and follow him?

6. *Read 6:27-49.* Describe a time when someone treated you or another person according to just one of the instructions by Jesus in 6:27-38. What was it like? Corrie Ten Boom

7. Jesus' point was not to provide his followers with a new rule book, a list of dos and don'ts you could mark off one by one, and sit back satisfied at the end of a successful moral day. Rather, what kind of heart and spirit was Jesus seeking to inculcate in his followers?

Actions from love; empathy

8. How would you like your heart and spirit to be more like the kind Jesus seeks?

9. This list of instructions is all about which God you believe in—and about the way of life that follows as a result. How does the God described by this list in verses 27-38 compare with your usual ideas about God?

10. Look at the four vivid word-sketches in 6:39-45 (the blind leading the blind, the student and the teacher, the speck and the plank, and the good and bad trees). How does each offer a "solution" that leaves the depths of the problem untouched?

Focus on being the best you

11. In the context of these four word-sketches and the whole chapter, what is Jesus saying through the story of the wise and foolish builders?

"Bedrock"

12. In what areas of your life are you so focused on looking for specks in
    other people's eyes that you miss them in your own?

    Blame Jim, not shouldering
    "my shore"

PRAY

The best response to the instructions of Jesus in the new kingdom may
be confession. Spend some time in quiet and personal reflection, con-
fessing to the Lord our failure to live out the Beatitudes and our pre-
occupation with other people's "planks."

8

True Faith

Luke 7

The stories that begin this chapter of Luke do two things in particular as Luke's larger narrative develops. They take the commands of the great sermon in chapter 6 and show what this life looks like on the ground, with God's love going out in new, unexpected, healing generosity.

And they prepare us for the question that is now emerging as the central one. Who does Jesus think he is? We will see how these stories further highlight his role, vocation and mission.

OPEN

What is something that you are dreading in the upcoming week, month or year? What are your emotions when you think of this task, event or experience? *Straightening up. Downsizing*

STUDY

1. *Read Luke 7:1-17.* A centurion is a Roman military office set in charge of about a hundred soldiers. What do we learn about the centurion in verses 1-10? What is he like? *Caring*

2. Normally in the Gospels Jesus does and says things that surprise people; this is one of the few places where Jesus himself is surprised. What is it that is so surprising to Jesus?

   What a non-Jew recognizes authority from God

3. How can the centurion's words to Jesus in verses 6-8 be a challenging model for our prayers?

   humble but faith filled

4. Put yourself in the story in verses 11-17 alongside the townspeople, those carrying the body, relatives and friends, the widow, the disciples. What do you see, hear and feel?

   Concern, sad

5. The centurion's servant was healed because of his owner's faith. Where is faith in the story in verses 11-17?

   Jesus offers the gift to build faith

6. What do these first two stories in chapter 7 say about Jesus' role, vocation and mission?

   Show God's love & care.

7. Think through the scene in verses 11-17 again, but this time, instead of a funeral, imagine the upcoming task or event you thought of in the opening question. Now imagine that Jesus enters that scene. What difference does it make for you?

   Comfort,

8. *Read 7:18-50*. John, in prison for being perceived to be a royal threat, is puzzled. If Jesus really is the Messiah, why isn't he establishing the sort of messianic kingdom John wants—presumably including liberation for prisoners like himself? Jesus is far too astute, with listening ears all around, to say openly, "Yes, I'm the Messiah." We hear a few chapters later that Herod wants to kill him, and a clear statement would have been an unnecessary risk. Instead, he heals all sorts of people before the eyes of the messengers, and suggests that they draw their conclusions—with a helping shove in the right direction provided by the quotation of various passages of Isaiah.

   How does Jesus use the images in 7:18-28 to question the expectations the Jews had of a king and a kingdom?

9. Looking at 7:29-35, how does the children's song (v. 32) illustrate the Pharisees' attitude toward John on the one hand and toward Jesus on the other?

   Complaints for any reason

10. In the story of Simon and the sinful woman (vv. 36-50), what we think of as "private life" in the modern Western world was largely unknown in Jesus' time. Doors would often remain open, allowing beggars, extra friends or simply curious passers-by to wander in. So the woman enters, it seems, with the intention of anointing Jesus.

    What do we learn about Simon, the woman and Jesus in this story?

11. In what ways does this story reverse the normal expectations of what would happen when God brought in his kingdom?

12. As you look back over this entire chapter, how does Luke define true faith?

PRAY

Consider which character in these various stories you identify with. Think about what Jesus might be saying to you as this character. Take time in prayer to allow Jesus to approach you, speak, touch and command. Sit in silence and listen to his words to you.

NOTE ON LUKE 7:24-28

What does Jesus mean by the reed he refers to in 7:24? When Herod Antipas chose the symbols for his coins, just a few years before the time of Jesus' public ministry, his favorite was a typical Galilean reed. You would see whole beds of them swaying in the breeze by the shores of the Sea of Galilee. A reed would have symbolized the beauty and fertility of that area. The reference to people who wear fine clothes and live in palaces also points his listeners to Herod.

So when Jesus in 7:28 talks about there being no one greater than John, he still has Herod in mind—contrasting these two prominent figures. But he does so, once again, in an indirect way so that no one can take it back as a hostile report to Herod. Those who sat down and chewed on it would realize, however, what was being said.

A SOWER AND A STORM

Luke 8:1-25

Many of Jesus' hearers were expecting something big and obvious when the kingdom of God arrived. They expected a new king to overthrow Herod, a new and legitimate priest to oust the present high priest, and in particular a Jewish movement to get rid of the hated pagans who were their ultimate masters. None of that was happening, certainly not in the way they thought.

In chapter 8, through a parable and in a storm, Jesus is keen to open their eyes and ears to see and hear what God was actually doing.

OPEN

What kind of storms have you run into in your life?

STUDY

1. *Read Luke 8:1-15.* Think about the characters we have met so far in Luke (Zechariah and Mary, Simeon and Anna, John the Baptist and

Herod, tax collectors and soldiers, villagers in Nazareth and villagers in Capernaum, Pharisees and teachers, the centurion and the widow, Simon and the sinful woman, the disciples and various other women, a leper and possessed man, and so forth).

How does the parable of the sower offer an overview of Jesus' ministry with these various kinds of people?

All have been exposed, few have taken hold & grown.

2. In verses 1-3, Luke includes a group of women whom the other Gospel writers don't mention until much later, not until the cross. What would first-century Palestinians have found shocking about these women? *Had money of their own.*

3. What seems to be the attraction of these women to Jesus?

He has healed

4. How do you see the Word producing growth and fruit in your own life?

Occasionally I see the connection. It's always touching.

5. Now think about the people around you at work and where you live. What kinds of soil would you say they represent and why?

Lots of thorny soil in our culture Distractions, worries, riches, etc.

6. What can we do to plough up the rough ground, to remove the stones, to weed out the thorns and sow the Word more successfully with people today? *Encourage & Support with love those who face challenges (testing). Focus on how to handle choking weeds*

7. *Read 8:16-25.* In a peasant culture like the one of Jesus' day, loyalty to family is extremely important. Mark's Gospel (3:21) tells us Jesus' family was afraid he was out of his mind. John's Gospel (7:5) explains they didn't believe him. Luke offers no such explanation. All we have is an apparently normal visit from the family, and Jesus' stunning reaction.

   Describe the shock waves that Jesus would have sent through his followers and the whole society with his response to the sudden request from his family. *Rude*
   Proclaiming a bigger family, new definition.

8. Exaggeration to make a point was common in Jesus' day as it is today in ordinary conversation among Middle Easterners. Jesus isn't saying that family has no or little importance. Rather, what is his point?
   Rude

9. Where do you hear the echoes of the parable of the sower in verses 16-21? *Light in place of seed.*

10. How does the story of the disciples in the boat (8:22-25) fit in with the truths and lessons of the previous twenty-one verses in this chapter?

God does the unexpected, Jesus is with us.

11. Luke outlines for us that the choice of faith is absolute. Either we trust Jesus or we are left at the mercy of the storm. We will only give the right answer to the question of who Jesus is when we realize that to give it commits us to total trust and obedience.

In what areas do you find it easy and difficult to trust Jesus and give him your obedience.

PRAY

Spend time praying to become good soil for the word of God and in response to question eleven. Pray for the faith and trust to give Jesus complete obedience in order to produce good fruit.

NOTE ON LUKE 8:10

Why wouldn't Jesus want people to hear and understand what he was saying? Jesus has already challenged the authorities and others regarding their ideas of who God's kingdom is for and how forgiveness of sins should take place, about having table fellowship with sinners and who is in charge of the sabbath, and much more. Many were looking for an opportunity to shut him up one way or another. Clear statements about his purpose would create an unnecessary risk. Better for those who truly want to know what he means, who truly want to hear, to come and ask him privately. For the rest, well, being a bit indirect is probably the best strategy for the moment. The time will come soon enough, as he suggests in 8:16-17, for what is hidden to be put on full display.

NOTE ON LUKE 8:16-21

We are shocked by Jesus' words about and response to his family. Is Jesus acting like a careless businessman who neglects his family because he is so focused on the next big deal? No, Jesus is making a "how much more" comparison, as is often found in the Gospels. While family was incredibly important to first-century Jews (and rightly so!), even family does not trump the absolute claim God has on our lives. Jesus is not denigrating family. He is elevating God's call on us. He is like the most caring family person you can imagine who nevertheless knows that hearing and doing God's word is even more important. This is no excuse for careerism or selfish attention to "my work." Yet Jesus knew that although his family didn't understand his vocation (though hoping they would in time), he couldn't allow them to distract or divert him from the vital and urgent mission he was undertaking.

WHOLENESS AND HOPE

Luke 8:26–9:17

We don't know for sure that Luke was a doctor, though there are several things in his work that make it likely, as well as Paul's mention of him as "Luke, the beloved doctor" (Colossians 4:14). But if he was, there must have been a wry smile on his face when he wrote in chapter 8 about a woman who had spent all she had on doctors without any cure.

What Luke points to in all the stories we are about to look at is that Jesus was not afraid to get his hands dirty with the problems people face. Jesus quietly but purposively came alongside those with difficulties and muddles, some which outwardly may have seemed impossible to deal with.

OPEN

Consider a time when you were asked to do something that was intimidating or frightening to you. How did you respond to that request?

STUDY

1. *Read Luke 8:26-39.* This incident took place on the eastern side of the lake, though exactly where is still a point of disagreement. For most of that shoreline the land does indeed steeply rise from close to the water. In any case, the area was largely Gentile territory, although many Jews would have lived there as well.

   Why might Jesus have decided to go there, across the lake from the main, predominantly Jewish, part of Galilee?

2. Describe the different reactions to Jesus in 8:26-39.

   Jesus remains calm before this human storm, as he had before the wind and waves on the lake. The same quiet authority will deal with the one as with the other. The bizarre scene with the pigs (another sign of Gentile territory; Jews didn't eat or keep pigs) has sometimes been seen as picture-language for what many Jews, and other inhabitants of the region, wanted to do with the hated foreign Romans—drive them back into the sea. To dismiss a regiment or squadron or legion of Roman soldiers in that way was the dream of several revolutionary leaders of the first century. But Luke's focus is on the man himself and, as always, on Jesus.

3. Why do you think the healed man longed to stay with Jesus?

4. In 8:39 what's the significance of the difference between what Jesus
    told the man to do and what he actually did?

5. *Read 8:40-56.* What are the similarities and differences between the
    two stories in these verses?

6. Here we see further signs of Luke caring about and being interested
    in the stories of women—unusual for someone writing in a very
    traditional society. Looking back on the first eight chapters of Luke,
    what other examples give evidence of this?

7. How are wholeness and hope seen in all three stories in 8:26-56?

8. A first-century reader coming upon this double story of Jairus's
    daughter and the bleeding woman would know very well that Je-
    sus was, apparently, incurring double pollution. In the first case he
    couldn't help it; the woman came and touched him without his know-
    ing either that she was doing it or what she was suffering from—but
    officially he had become "unclean" nonetheless. In the second case,

though, Jesus deliberately went and touched a dead body.

Already in these instances we see the same pattern emerging. Jesus shares the pollution of sickness and death, but the power of his own love—and it is love, above all, that shines through in these stories—turns that pollution into wholeness and hope. It is the presence of Jesus, getting his hands dirty with the problems of the world, that we are promised in the gospel.

In what muddle or fear, suffering or problem do you need Jesus to come alongside you?

9. *Read 9:1-17.* What might be the purpose of sending the disciples into ministry with these restrictions?

    They must depend on the Lord God
    to provide. Growing trust & prayer

10. Jesus then makes the apparently outrageous request of the disciples that they feed the crowd. How is what Jesus does next (or what Jesus does with the few loaves and fish) a sharply focused version of what they themselves had just been doing as they traveled around?

11. What is Luke's point in inserting the comment about Herod here (9:7-9) between these two episodes?

    Establishment is anxious

12. Christians who intend to make the gospel story their own are living a venture of faith from first to last. Not, however, blind faith. We aren't called to believe that Jesus can, as it were, do tricks to order. He wasn't a magician. What he did on this rare occasion was to allow God's creative power to flow through him in a special way, as with his healings, only more so. And, as the Gospel writers describe this incident with words so familiar in the later church from celebrations of the Lord's Supper (he "took the bread, blessed it, broke it and gave it"), we Christians are invited to invoke that same healing, creative power in all that we do, in everything that flows from our life of worship.

Jesus brought together meeting the needs of others and worship. Where do you sense God inviting you to participate in his healing, creative work?

PRAY

Take some time to sit in silence with Jesus and picture him coming alongside you in the area of struggle or suffering from question eight. What is he saying to you? Ask that he will guide you and help you depend on him to provide what you need as you seek to join Jesus in the work he does to help others.

11

THE NATURE
OF DISCIPLESHIP

Luke 9:18-62

The Oscar-winning movie *Chariots of Fire* tells the story of two athletes at the 1924 Paris Olympics. Harold Abrahams, after a gigantic struggle as much against himself as against the other runners, achieved the gold medal in the 100 meters. Eric Liddell, the devout Christian who had refused to run on a Sunday, switched events and won the gold in the 400 meters.

After the Games were over, the movie shows all the athletes returning on the boat train to London, and spilling out excitedly into Waterloo station. All except Harold Abrahams. Only when the crowds have gone does Harold emerge slowly from the train. He has achieved what he set out to do. He has the long-coveted prize in his hand. He has been to the mountain, and is realizing that whatever he does now he will never stand there again. He has to come down from the giddy heights and face reality.

OPEN

Describe an event in your life that could be characterized as a "mountaintop" experience.

STUDY

1. *Read Luke 9:18-27.* Think about what the disciples have seen and learned already in being with Jesus. What would have contributed to the answer Peter gives?

2. Why should it come as no surprise that Jesus tells those who want to follow him that there is a dark and dangerous time ahead?

3. How does the message of Jesus in verses 23-26 contradict much of what we hear today about the Christian life and what it means to follow Jesus?

4. Jesus says those who follow him must pick up their cross. How have you seen sacrifice and suffering be part of following Jesus?

5. *Read 9:28-45.* When Jesus' appearance is changed, or transfigured, he is discussing with Moses and Elijah his departure, which he was going to fulfill in Jerusalem. The word for "departure" is *exodus*. This can simply mean "going away," or it can serve as a euphemism for his death. Of course the word also hearkens back to when Moses led the people of Israel out of Egypt as described in the book of Exodus.

   What parallels are there between the original exodus of Israel from Egypt and Jesus' death on the cross?

6. Why does Jesus seem to shift quickly from asking the disciples who
   they think he is to summoning them to follow him, even to death?

7. All of the Gospel writers follow the story of the transfiguration with
   the story of a boy who is desperately ill, so sick that the disciples
   cannot cure him. How do these two stories go together?

8. The more open we are to God, and to the different dimensions of
   God's glory, the more we seem to be open to the pain of the world.
   In what ways have you seen this truth in your own life?

9. *Read 9:46-62.* How are the interchanges of verses 46-50 ironic in
   light of what Jesus has just told the disciples in verse 44?

10. Jews would regularly make pilgrimages to Jerusalem (as we saw Je-
    sus' parents do in 2:41). While this wasn't the moment yet for an offi-
    cial pilgrimage to Jerusalem, the destination introduced in 9:31 now
    (in 9:51) becomes Jesus' goal. From this point on Jesus is constantly
    on the move, and this journey will continue—providing a frame for
    most of Luke's Gospel—until 19:41.

    How do verses 51-62 show what Jesus' journey *will* be like and what
    it *will not* be like?

11. When they start, Jesus sends messengers (the word can also mean "angels") ahead of him. Luke wants to remind us that this is indeed an exodus journey. In the book of Exodus itself (23:20) God "sends his angel before you" to guide the people into the land. But this is also a new exodus journey; the prophet Malachi (3:1) declares that God will send his angel, or messenger, before him, so that when he arrives to judge and save, the people will be ready. All James and John can think of is that they are now in the same position as Elijah in the Old Testament. If they meet opposition, they want to call down fire from heaven (2 Kings 1:10-12).

In what ways are the people that Jesus meets on the road like the seed sown on rocky ground or among thorns, in Luke 8?

12. As you think about your journey of faith, when you are tempted to look back instead of move forward, what helps you move forward?

PRAY

Offer to God your doubts or fears about where Jesus is asking you to travel. Wait for him to point out places where you are tempted to look back when you should be looking ahead.

Breaking Boundaries, Bringing Peace

Luke 10

The world knows (or should know) what Archbishop Desmond Tutu achieved in South Africa through the Truth and Reconciliation Commission. When the racist policies of apartheid ended in South Africa and Nelson Mandela was elected president in the 1990s, the Commission, headed by Tutu, heard white security forces and black guerillas both confess in public their violent and horrific crimes during the repressive period of South Africa's recent history.

The fact of such a body even existing, let alone doing the work it has done, is the most extraordinary sign of the power of the Christian gospel in the world in my lifetime. We only have to think for a moment of how unthinkable such a thing would have been twenty-five years before, or indeed how unthinkable such a thing would still be in Beirut, Belfast or (God help us) Jerusalem, to see that something truly remarkable has taken place for which we should thank God in fear and trembling.

When barriers are broken down, when those who were previously enemies are reconciled, it is truly a work of God.

OPEN

What barriers and boundaries do you observe in the culture around you, in your community, even in your church?

STUDY

1. *Read Luke 10:1-24.* In this instance of Jesus sending out his disciples (vv. 1-16), what clues in the text reveal that their mission is a matter of real urgency? *Travel light, Keep moving*

2. How does Jesus express in verses 3-9 that peace is at the heart of his message? *It's the first thing to say,*

3. What is the invitation and the warning found in the message that the disciples are sent out with?
   the Kingdom of God is near.

Jesus' contemporaries were for the most part not wanting peace—not peace with their traditional enemies the Samaritans nor peace with the feared and hated Romans. They wanted an all-out war that would bring God's justice swiftly to their aid and get rid of their enemies once and for all. But Jesus' vision of God's kingdom was going in the opposite direction. It grew directly out of his knowledge and love of Israel's God as the God of generous grace and astonishing, powerful, healing love.

The judgment that would fall on Chorazin and Bethsaida in central Galilee, and on Jesus' own town of Capernaum, would be more terrible than that suffered by the wicked cities of the Old Testament. But it would not consist of fire falling from heaven. It would take the form of Roman invasion and destruction. Rome's punishment for rebel subjects would be the direct result of God's people turning away from God's way of peace. This of course is what actually happened about thirty-five years later in response to Israel's rising use of violence against Rome.

The seventy Jesus sent were not offering people a new religious option which might have a gentle effect on their lives. They were holding out the last chance for people to turn away from Israel's flight into ruin, and to accept God's way of peace.

4. Rome is a power to be reckoned with. And there are right ways and wrong ways to respond. But behind and above that power is the ultimate enemy.

    On return of the seventy, what does Jesus celebrate (vv. 17-24)?

    The work that God did. God is known to those humble & willing.

5. What emerges then in these verses as God's primary purposes?

6. *Read 10:25-42.* The lawyer's question about the key requirements for entering the age to come was a standard rabbinic question to which there were standard answers, one of which Jesus calls on the lawyer to recite. But not wanting to look like he was merely asking an obvious question with an obvious answer, the lawyer goes further. Jesus responds with a story about one of the hated Samaritans.

   The lawyer's question in verse 29 and Jesus' answer in verse 36 don't quite match up. What's the difference?

   Neighbor" is not defined by state of the recipient. "Neighbor" is defined by the spiritual/mental attitude of the actor.

7. How does Jesus' story reinforce his message about the importance of the way of peace?

8. What is at stake, then and now, is the question of whether we will use the God-given revelation of love and grace as a way of boosting our own sense of isolated security and purity, or whether we will see it as a call and challenge to extend that love and grace to the whole world.

   What barriers exist between your faith community and others?

9. What is one way, large or small, that you could break through this barrier and begin to dismantle the isolated security of your faith community?

10. Jesus moves from one boundary-breaking episode with the lawyer to another in the story of Mary and Martha. In Jewish culture to sit at someone's feet meant to be their student, not to exhibit a devoted, doglike adoring posture. (Thus Saul was said to have "sat at the feet of Gamaliel" in Acts 22:3.) To sit at the feet of a rabbi was what you did *if you wanted to be a rabbi yourself.*

    In this context of a very traditional culture, why would Martha have found Mary's actions so shocking and objectionable?

11. Jesus affirms Mary's right to be his student. How does this further extend Jesus' agenda of peace, of breaking down barriers between separated groups?

12. What are ways your Christian community can break down the barriers of privilege or tension that might be found between men and women?

PRAY

Spend time in praise over the boundary-breaking call and power of Jesus. Give thanks for the ways in which Jesus has broken barriers in your own life and in your community. Finish by praying for the courage to step out and live out this call in your community.

NOTE ON LUKE 10:18

The word *satan* literally means "accuser," and "the satan" appears in Scripture as the director of public prosecutions in God's heavenly council (Job 1:6-12; 2:1-7; Zechariah 3:1-2). At some point he seems to have overstepped the role, not only bringing unfounded accusations, but inciting people to do things for which he can then accuse them. Finally, in flagrant rebellion against God and his plans of salvation for the world, the satan seeks to pervert, distort and overthrow Israel, the chosen bearers of God's promise, and to turn aside from his task Israel's true Messiah, the bringer of fulfillment. He has gained enormous power because the world in general, and Israel's leaders too, have been tricked by his cunning. Jesus' task is to defeat the satan, to break his power, to win the decisive victory which will open the way to God's new creation in which evil, and even death itself, will be banished.

13

WARNINGS AND WOES

Luke 11

The great church is completely dark. It is almost midnight, and the little crowd outside the west door shuffles round and stamps to keep warm in the chilly April air. Then, as the clock strikes, the fire is lit, with a sudden glow on all the watching faces. A single candle is lit from the fire. The doors swing open, the light moves forward into the pitch-black church, and the Easter celebration begins. Soon the whole place will be full of flickering, glowing candlelight, the light of God's power and love shining in the darkness of the world.

Not every church celebrates Easter this way, but the example helps make sense of the confusing collection of sayings in this passage. Light brings hope and new possibility, but it also brings judgment. Jesus, on his way to Jerusalem, is constantly saying in one way or another that God's light will shine out and expose the darkness that had taken hold of the hearts and minds of his contemporaries.

OPEN

What warning from Jesus do you think the church today most needs to hear again and heed?

STUDY

1. *Read Luke 11:1-13.* The laws of hospitality in the ancient Middle East were strict, and if a traveler arrived needing food and shelter, one was under an obligation to provide it.

   There are all sorts of ways in which God is not like the sleepy friend, but on what point of comparison is Jesus focusing?

2. What does the example of God as father in these verses teach about the character of God?

3. How does the prayer in these verses also describe what Jesus is seeking to accomplish?

4. *Read 11:14-54.* What might have been the reasons that Jesus' opponents launch this attack on him in verses 14-28?

5. Describe the fatal flaw in the opponents' logic that Jesus points out throughout verses 14-28.

6. Jesus says what he is doing is "by the finger of God"—a phrase that will remind his listeners of the powerful works which Moses did at Pharaoh's court (Exodus 8:19). Jesus is showing that the God of the Exodus is alive and well and at work in him. His journey to Jerusalem is marked at every step by signs of what he must accomplish there. The power which enables him to defeat the demons in the present is the same power by which, through death itself, he will destroy death. For the moment, though, a warning.

   What is the warning that Jesus gives in verses 24-28, not to an individual, but to the nation?

7. How does Jesus continue his warnings to Israel in verses 29-36?

8. In what ways do the verses about light (vv. 33-36) go beyond speaking of a general wisdom or spiritual illumination?

9. The last phrase in verse 41 literally means, "give for alms those things that are inside." If Jesus meant by this something such as "give over to God for his use" it becomes much clearer. According to the exchange between Jesus and the Pharisee in verses 37-41, what does it mean to live like this?

10. Jesus is not just saying he is irritated with the Pharisees. What is at the heart of all the "woes" that Jesus proclaims in verses 42-54?

11. Jesus saw clearly that there were many self-appointed teachers in the world of first-century Judaism who were using their learning partly for their own political and theological ends. In what ways do we see this same pattern in our society today?

12. Where do you see the tendency in your own life to hold firmly to ideas, political views or other agendas that are not consistent with Jesus' message of peace and light for the world?

PRAY

Use the prayer time as an opportunity for repentance. Jesus called the Pharisees and religious leaders to an agenda of repentance from their flight into national rebellion against Rome and their theological rebellion against God. Confess the areas of rebellion in your own life.

NOTE ON LUKE 11:24-26

Jesus tells a strange story about an evil spirit which returns to the place it left. This can't be a warning about the likely effect of exorcisms; if it was, it would be better not to do them at all, since the poor person ends up worse off than before. It probably means what it seems to in Matthew (12:43-45), applying not to an individual person but to the nation as a whole.

The point of Jesus' exorcisms, after all, was not simply to heal as many individuals as possible. If that were his aim, he wasn't very successful when seen in the longer term. Rather, he was aiming to enact God's kingdom, for Israel and the world. Israel, like a demon-possessed person, had been "cleansed" by various movements of reform. But unless the living presence of God came to dwell in its midst, Israel would remain vulnerable to the return of demons. Jesus stood there among his people, embodying the return of God to Israel. Unless they turned from accusation to acceptance, the demons that had led them to ruin in former days would come back in full force.

14

JESUS' CALL
TO WATCHFULNESS

Luke 12

There is a shift in the book of Luke between the early chapters and the section we begin in chapter 12. Luke is allowing his readers to see how, with Jesus on the long road to Jerusalem, tension is building up, opposition is becoming stronger, and anyone who wants to follow Jesus is going to have to become focused, totally loyal, ready for anything.

The mood now is not so much "religious" as it is like the concentrated campaign of someone running for high office in a country where political opponents and their supporters will literally come to blows, and perhaps try to imprison or impeach one another. What Jesus is doing demands total attention. Anything less, and disaster may follow.

OPEN

Describe an example of a person who was (or is) totally loyal to someone or something.   SS

STUDY

1. *Read Luke 12:1-34.* Who are the enemies mentioned explicitly and implicitly in verses 1-12, and why is only one worth fearing?

   the evil one who/that can destroy our eternal soul

2. Why, in contrast, does Jesus say the disciples are not to fear God?

3. In the context of this dangerous political and spiritual climate, what is the significance of what Jesus says in verses 2-3 and 8-12 about the words the disciples speak?   *political i*

   2-3 God knows? other will repeat
   8/10 - forgiven
   11-12 God provides word in trying moments

   In the midst of these verses comes a dire warning which many people have found disturbing. One may be forgiven for speaking against the Son of Man, but will not be forgiven for blaspheming against the Holy Spirit. In Matthew and Mark this saying occurs when Jesus has been accused of casting out demons by the power of the prince of demons. Here in Luke 12 the intention seems broader. Someone who sees Jesus at work and misunderstands what is going on may speak against him only to discover the truth and repent. But if someone denounces the work of the Spirit, such a person is cut off by that very action from profiting from that work. Once you declare that the spring of fresh water is in fact polluted, you will never drink from it. The one sure thing about this saying is that if someone is anxious about having committed the sin against the Holy Spirit, their anxiety is a clear sign that they have not.

4. With trust in God on the one hand, and the desperate nature of the battle on the other, Jesus' followers must stand by him steadfastly. The warnings about dangerous foes, and the promise that our God knows and cares about the smallest details of our lives, combine to challenge us against a casual, half-hearted, relaxed Christianity.

What does it mean for us today to live with dedicated, single-minded discipleship?

Be aware of God's presence constantly.

5. What are the similarities and differences between the greed and anxiety of Jesus' day (discussed in verses 13-34) and the greed and anxiety exhibited today?

We imagine that today's culture is more greedy, more anxious because of instant/constant media attn.

6. In verses 22-34 Jesus isn't asking the disciples to reflect on the birds and flowers to encourage a kind of romantic nature-mysticism. What is his point instead?

God cares about all of His creation but especially us.

7. How does Jesus challenge your thinking about possessions, security and God's rule in this life?

Hold this temporary dwelling place with a loose hand.

8. *Read 12:35-59.* Not only is Jesus engaged in a running battle with the powers of evil. Not only is he issuing a challenge for total loyalty in the face of opposition. Not only is he saying that God's kingdom now demands a complete reordering of priorities. He is now warning that a crisis is coming, a great showdown for which one must be prepared. And his warnings in this passage begin with advice that was originally given to the Israelites for the keeping of the first Passover before their sudden exodus from Egypt (Exodus 12:11). As we have seen, Luke highlights the exodus theme at various points in his story of Jesus' journey to Jerusalem, and the passage in question here points particularly to the first keeping of Passover. The Israelites were to eat that meal already dressed for their journey, so that they could be up and off at a moment's notice.

    In verses 35-48 what does it mean for the disciples to be "ready"?

9. Peter's question in verse 41 is an important one. Do you think this picture of the master coming back home refers just to the disciples or also to Israel as a whole? Why do you think that?

10. Being entrusted with ministry is an awesome responsibility, and one to which the picture of the servants and master applies quite well. How can verses 35-48 also be applied to those with responsibilities in the community of believers?

11. In what ways do verses 49-53 challenge common understandings of what the gospel is all about?

12. What relevance might the warnings from verses 54-59 have for us, living nearly two thousand years after the events happened that Jesus is referring to?

PRAY

Pray that God's people will be able to read the signs of the times, the great movements of people, governments, nations and policies—and act accordingly as God's people. Pray for the trust to lay down the anxieties or desires that affect our single-minded discipleship in such a world.

NOTE ON LUKE 12:33-34

The final appeal, which will be repeated at various stages late in Luke, is not necessarily for all followers of Jesus to get rid of all their possessions. Luke himself, in Acts, describes Christian communities in which most members live in their own houses with their own goods around them, and there is no suggestion that they are second-class or rebellious members of God's people. Jesus is returning to the sharing of inheritance with which the passage began, and is advocating the opposite attitude to the grasping and greed which he saw there.

When he speaks of "treasure in heaven," here and elsewhere, this doesn't mean treasure that you will only possess after death. "Heaven" is God's sphere of created reality, which, as the Lords' Prayer suggests, will one day colonize "earth," our sphere, completely. What matters is that the kingdom of God is bringing the values and priorities of God himself to bear on the greed and anxiety of the world. Those who welcome Jesus and his kingdom-message must learn to abandon the latter and live by the former.

15

ENTERING THROUGH THE NARROW DOOR

Luke 13

Chapter 13 begins with an incident that illustrates Pontius Pilate's frequently cruel and offensive behavior toward the Jewish people. There are many historical references to the ways in which Pilate crushed rebellions and flouted the laws and conventions of the Jewish people. Chapter 13 refers to a group of Galileans on a pilgrimage who were offering sacrifices in the temple when Pilate, perhaps fearing rebellion, slaughtered them. Their blood was mixed with the blood of their sacrifices—polluting the temple on top of the human horror and tragedy of the event.

Consequently, when people bring the news of this event to Jesus they are not just telling a shocking story. Two questions hover in the air as they recount the events. First, does Jesus really intend to continue his journey (at the head of a Galilean pilgrimage)? And second, what does this mean? Is this the beginning of something worse? If Jesus has been warning of woe and disaster coming on those who refuse his message, is this a sign that these Galileans were already being punished?

Jesus' stern comments throughout the chapter address both questions.

OPEN

Daily we hear of violence in the world, and sometimes quite nearby. How does violence so often beget more violence?

Vengeance

STUDY

1. *Read Luke 13:1-21.* In verses 1-5 Jesus isn't calling for repentance because of what happens to people after they die. Instead, considering the immediate context of Pilate's actions, what does he mean by "in the same way," and what kind of repentance would avoid this fate?

   Luke 12:4-5 —

   Jesus also says that buildings might come down on people as happened with the tower in Siloam (a small area of Jerusalem just to the south of the temple itself). While accidents do happen, Jesus' point is that those who refuse his summons to change direction, to abandon the crazy flight into national rebellion against Rome, will find the very walls collapsing on top of them as the enemy closes in.

2. In the Old Testament, a fig tree was often used to symbolize the nation of Israel (for example, in Hosea 9:10), something Jesus' listeners would have recognized. How does the parable of the fig tree in verses 6-9 amplify the warning Jesus has been giving?

   Jesus is perhaps "buying a stay of execution"

3. There are two ways of taking this parable, both of which give a satis-
    factory meaning and arrive at the same point. How can Jesus be seen
    as either the vineyard owner or as the gardener?

    Both — trinity in play

4. The tension in this parable is whether or not Jerusalem will repent
    and be rescued. The question for today is, What is God up to in our
    world today and in our own lives? In what ways can we bear the fruit
    of repentance called for by the kingdom of God?

    bearing fruit

5. In verses 10-17 there's more than one power struggle going on in the
    synagogue. Describe each.

    struggle betw Jesus & evil spirit
    Jesus & synagogue ruler

6. In what ways is Jesus doing for this woman what he longs to do for
    Israel as a whole?

    Given health, joy

7. How does Luke use the little sayings in verses 18-21 to comment on
    what has just happened in the synagogue?

    Kingdom starts w/ small matters

8. *Read Luke 13:22-35.* In the context of Jesus' journey to Jerusalem, "being saved" is not simply a matter of ultimate destination after death, but the immediate and pressing question of the crisis that hangs over the nation. *Spared lives in conflict*

   In verses 22-30, what is Jesus' stern warning to Israel?

   Urgent to repent & turn to God

9. What is significant about what these verses say about the Gentiles, the very people whom Jesus' contemporaries were eager to fight and who had bullied and oppressed the Jewish people for centuries?

   Non Israelis come to Gods table

10. We should be cautious about lifting Luke 13:22-30 out and applying it directly to the larger question of eternal salvation. Jesus' urgent warnings to his own contemporaries were aimed at the particular emergency they then faced. But we should equally beware of assuming that it is irrelevant to such questions. Unless all human life is just a game; unless we are mistaken in our strong sense that our moral and spiritual choices matter; unless, after all, the New Testament as a whole has badly misled us—then it really is possible to stroll past the open gate to the kingdom of God, only to discover later the depth of our mistake.

    What is the warning in this section for us today?

11. In verses 31-35 news of a threat from Herod prompts Jesus to muse on his work and how it will be completed. The image in verse 34 is

of a fire in a farmyard. Animals have developed ways of protecting their young in situations where they can't escape. There are stories of exactly this picture, where a hen will be found dead, scorched from a fire, but her chicks will still be alive under her wings.

How do verses 32-33 and the image of the hen combine to tell us what Jesus thinks his death is all about?

12. How are you affected by this picture of Jesus as the hen who gives her life for her chicks?

PRAY

Pray for our world, so full of violence and reliance on power. Pray that we will find a better path by putting our trust in God and obeying him.

Spend time in praise and thanksgiving as well for the incredible grace of the Lord Jesus. He opened the narrow door for all people and has given his life for all. Then, pray that your life would bear fruit in accordance with this grace, that your community of faith would show in practical ways that they have been brought from "east and west, from north and south," to share in the feast in the kingdom of God.

NOTE ON LUKE 13:31

The Pharisees here, who warn Jesus of Herod's intentions, may have been among the many moderate Pharisees who, like Gamaliel in Acts 5, were happy to watch from the sidelines and see whether or not this new movement turned out to be from God. They may, of course, have been secretly hoping to get rid of Jesus, to get him off their territory, but Luke gives no hint of that if it was so.

16

THE GREAT BANQUET

Luke 14

Luke's Gospel has more mealtime scenes than all the others. If his vision of the Christian life, from one point of view, is a journey, from another point of view it's a party. Several stories end with a festive meal—like, for instance, the parable of the prodigal son in the next chapter. These themes come together in the Last Supper and, finally, the story of the road to Emmaus in chapter 24.

In chapter 14 Luke has brought together two parables about feasting. The first one in verses 7-11 is not always recognized as a parable, because it looks more like a piece of social advice or practical wisdom. But Jesus didn't come to offer good advice, and often his own conduct seems calculated to cause embarrassment. So we ought to expect this parable and the second one to have meanings beyond social advice.

OPEN

Describe the last party you attended or hosted. Who was invited? What were the people like who attended the party? How enjoyable was it for you?

STUDY

1. *Read Luke 14:1-35.* Looking at verses 1-11, in what ways do Jesus' conversation and parable address those in his day who were jostling for position in the eyes of God?

2. There is a wider meaning in these first fourteen verses for the first readers of Luke, who was writing perhaps forty years after Jesus' death. Thousands of non-Jews had become Christians—had entered, that is, into the dinner party prepared by the God of Abraham, Isaac, and Jacob. Many Jewish Christians had found this difficult to understand or approve. They were so eager to maintain their own places at the top table that they could not grasp God's design and grace for others.

   How can people in the church today exhibit a jostling for position like the Jewish Christians of Luke's day did?

3. The parable in verses 15-24 also speaks to those around Jesus, to those in the church in Luke's day and to the church today. How is the parable a description of what Jesus has been doing up to this point within Galilee?

4. What do you notice about the excuses people are giving for why they cannot attend the banquet?

5. While we can't press every detail of the parable too far, in what ways does this parable speak to the Jews and Gentiles in the church in Luke's day?

6. What does it mean for the church today to go out into the "streets and lanes of the town" in order to bring people into the banquet?

7. Why is this often difficult for us to do?

8. Moving on to verses 25-35, how does Jesus keep turning the world's values and common expectations upside down?

9. We could say that Jesus is engaging in typical Middle Eastern exaggeration to make his point about family and possessions. And that may be true. Nonetheless, what is his point?

10. The two pictures of the tower and the battle (14:28-32) also carried a cryptic warning in Jesus' day. The most important building project of his time was of course the temple in Jerusalem: Herod the Great had begun a massive program of rebuilding and beautifying it, and his sons and heirs were carrying on the work. But what was it all for? Would it ever be completed? In fact, Jesus has already warned

that God has abandoned his house (13:35); by A.D. 70 Herod's temple would be left a smoldering ruin by the Romans, its folly plain for all to see.

What specific warning does the picture of the battle then hold for Jesus' contemporaries?

11. How would Jesus' comments about salt in 14:34-35 have also applied to the nation of Israel?

12. When there is an urgent task to be done, then everything, including family, possessions and one's own life, must be put at risk. If Jesus' followers aren't ready to do that for the sake of the kingdom, then they are like the tower-builder and the warmonger who haven't thought through what they are really about.

What might costly discipleship in light of the urgency of the kingdom look like for you or your Christian community?

PRAY

Sit in silence and allow the Holy Spirit to speak to you about what might be keeping you from attending the banquet, or from costly discipleship. Then move on to praying about who you can invite to the banquet.

17

THE PARABLES
OF THE LOST

Luke 15

Imagine moving into a new house in a new neighborhood, and on the very first night you are there, a loud, chaotic party occurs down the street. Imagine the loud music, the amplified voices and the long hours of wondering if this was going to be a regular occurrence in your new neighborhood.

That kind of experience illustrates how one person's celebration can be really annoying for someone else, especially if they don't understand the reason for the party. The parables in Luke 15 are told because Jesus was making a habit of having celebration parties with all the "wrong" people, and some others thought this was a nightmare.

All three stories in chapter 15 are ways of saying, "This is why we're celebrating!" In and through these stories we all get a wide-open window on what Jesus thought he was doing—and, perhaps, on what we ourselves should be doing.

OPEN

Recall something you lost and were frustrated that you couldn't find.

What did it feel like when you were looking, and if you found it, how
did you react then? *Diamond*

STUDY

1. *Read Luke 15:1-32.* What problem do the Pharisees and the teachers
   of the law have with what Jesus had been doing (vv. 1-2)?

   unclean

2. What might Christians do today that would make people ask in surprise, "Why in the world are you doing that?" just as the Pharisees
   asked about Jesus' parties?

   Help people "just because"— even if they don't deserve, appreciate it

3. How do the stories of the lost sheep and the lost coin (vv. 3-10) illustrate the differences in what "repentance" meant to Jesus and to
   the Pharisees?

   The "lost" items aren't blamed.

4. What effect would these stories have had on the repentant sinners
   who heard them?

Melissa bronchitis

5. Looking at the next parable of the two sons, describe all the ways in which the younger son brings shame to his family just in verses 11-16.

6. What makes the father the most remarkable character in this story?

   Understanding both sons

7. Inside the story in verses 11-32 there is another dimension. One of the greatest stories in Israel's history is the exodus, when God brought them out of Egypt through Moses. Many years later the Israelites were sent into exile in Babylon after a long rebellion against God. Even though many Jews returned after the exile, many contemporaries of Jesus believed they were still living in virtual exile, though this time pagans were ruling over them in their own land. They looked for the time when a new exodus would liberate them from their social and spiritual exile and restore their freedom and fortunes.

   How does the story of the prodigal son echo Israel's story of exodus and exile?

   Self-imposed

8. Look closely at what the older brother says in verses 25-32. What do you notice in his language about his perspective and attitude?

9. In verses 25-32, what is Jesus' saying to his critics, the Pharisees and the teachers of the law?

10. In what ways does this parable point, for Luke, beyond the immediate situation of Jesus' ministry to the early church and the Gentiles and Jews within the church?

11. The story, of course, is unfinished. We naturally want to know if the older brother is persuaded by his father, if he is reconciled to his brother, how the younger brother behaves from now on. Of course, at this point in the Gospel, the story of Jesus and the Pharisees is unfinished as well. But sometimes a storyteller leaves much that is open-ended to invite us to consider how we fit in the story and what our response is.

   Which role in the final parable do you and your church find comes most naturally to you, and why?

12. How can we celebrate the party of God's love in such a way as to welcome not only the younger brothers who have come back from the dead but also the older brothers who thought there was nothing wrong with them?

PRAY

Spend some time repenting of your tendencies to be either the younger brother or the older brother. Then, finish your prayer time with praise and thanksgiving for the lavish, prodigal love of God the Father.

NOTE ON LUKE 15:1-2

The tax collectors were disliked not just because they collected taxes—nobody much likes them in any culture—but because they were collecting money for either Herod or the Romans, or both. And if they were in regular contact with Gentiles, some might have considered them unclean.

The "sinners" are a more general category, and people disagree as to who precisely they were. They may just have been people who were too poor to know the law properly or to try to keep it (see John 7:49). Certainly they were people who were regarded by the self-appointed experts as hopelessly irreligious, out of touch with the demands that God had made on Israel through the law.

NOTE ON LUKE 15:3-10

In the stories of the sheep and the coin, the punch line in each case depends on the Jewish belief that the two halves of God's creation, heaven and earth, were meant to fit together and be in harmony with each other. If you discover what's going on in heaven, you'll discover how things were meant to be on earth. That, after all, is the point of praying that God's kingdom will come "on earth as in heaven."

18

FAITHFULNESS
AND STEWARDSHIP

Luke 16

Wealth is a killer. About half the stories in the newspapers seem to be about money in one way or another—the glamour and glitz it seems to provide, the shock and the horror when it runs out, the never-ending scandals about people getting it, embezzling it, losing it and getting it again. Then there are the robberies, burglaries and the numerous other obvious ways in which money is at the center of simple, old-fashioned wrongdoing.

Luke begins this chapter with a parable about money, then moves to actual teaching about money, and the chapter will end with another parable in which money is both part of the story and part of the point. This passage contains some of Jesus' strongest and most explicit warnings about the dangers of wealth, and experience suggests that neither the church nor the world has taken these warnings sufficiently to heart.

Somewhere along the line serious repentance and a renewed determination to hear and obey Jesus' clear teaching seem called for.

OPEN

When you think of money, what comes to mind first?

What is your greatest struggle in regard to money?

STUDY

1. *Read Luke 16:1-31.* Jews were forbidden to lend money at interest, but many people got round this by lending in kind, with oil and wheat being easy commodities to use for this purpose. It is likely that what the steward did in verses 1-9 was deduct from the bill the interest that the master had been charging.

   That would leave just the principal to be paid back. The debtors would be delighted, but the master wouldn't. Nonetheless, he couldn't openly lay a charge against the steward without owning up to his own shady business practices. Thus when the master heard about what had happened, he couldn't help but admire the man's clever approach even though he suffered financially because of it.

   How does this cultural background information help your understanding of the story, and what questions remain for you?

2. What we have in verses 1-9 is a parable, not primarily straightforward moral teaching on money—though, as with the parables about

feasts in chapter 14, we find some moral teaching on the subject along the way. So, if we were faced with a first-century Jewish story about a master and a steward, we would likely identify the master as God and the steward as Israel. And that is the case here, in some (but not all) respects.

With this in mind, what situation is Jesus indicating that Israel is in, and what is he implying they should do?

3. Even though this parable appears to be directed specifically to the situation in Jesus' day, it can be reused in our own day. It has nothing to do with commending dishonest or underhanded practices in business or personal finance. Rather it recommends resourcefulness when circumstances call for it. It advises us to be flexible and not be too bound by unnecessary regulations that are over and above the gospel itself, especially not in the church.

    What critical situation is your faith community facing, and how might you be creative and flexible in meeting that state of affairs?

4. From a parable about money, Luke moves on in 16:10-18 to actual teaching about money. Here Jesus speaks of it as a trust. What difference does it make to view money as a trust rather than as a possession?

5. How would it look practically in your life if you treated your money and material goods as a trust?

6. As in most peasant societies, in Jesus' day there was a very small number of extremely rich people and a very large number of the very poor. The rich included the chief priests (some of their opulent houses in Jerusalem have been discovered by archaeologists), so any attack on the rich would include an attack on them. The Pharisees were more of a populist movement, but the danger they faced, with the land as a key part of their religion, was that they would equate possession of land, and the wealth it brought, with God's blessing. Jesus' stern warnings at the end of chapter 14 had already made it clear that this was not the way.

   The Pharisees might have pointed out that much in the Jewish law encouraged their view of possessions as a sign of God's favor. Jesus, of course, takes the opposite view, with much of the prophetic writings (as well as the law's commands for Israel to care for the poor and needy) clearly on his side. His relationship to the law, however, is not exactly straightforward.

   How do verses 16-18 reveal Jesus' view of the law and the prophets (the books we would call the Old Testament) as taking their place in a sequence of events within God's plan?

7. How are verses 10-18 all connected by the challenge of being faithful?

8. In the last part of the chapter, verses 19-31, we have a parable—and so again we know that it is not primarily a moral tale about riches and poverty. Neither should we press the details of the story too far to unearth information about life after death. Rather, since it is a parable, we should take it as picture-language about something that was going on in Jesus' own work.

   How does the story of the rich man and Lazarus function in this way?

9. What parallels and contrasts do you see between this story of Lazarus and the rich man, on the one hand, and the story of the prodigal son, on the other?

10. Jesus was not the first to tell of how wealth and poverty might be reversed in the future life. Stories like the one in verses 19-31 were so well known that what would have struck the hearers was how he changed the format. In such stories, generally the request to send someone back to warn family is granted.

   What effect would Jesus' change to the ending of his story have had on his audience?

11. In what ways does the very last sentence of the story, verse 31, speak to us?

12. What specific idea or verse from chapter 16 stands out most for you and why?

PRAY

Take the prayer time to be in communication with God. Spend a few moments in quiet prayer reflecting on the truths of the passage or asking God for clarity in your own life about faithfulness, money and the meaning of the resurrection.

19

FAITH AND THE KINGDOM

Luke 17

What does the word *apocalypse* conjure up for you? Stars falling from the sky, volcanoes and earthquakes? People in terror, panicking and rushing this way and that? The Bible has plenty of apocalypses, and sometimes they sound like that. The second half of this passage is one of them. But did Jesus think it would be like that?

The rest of Luke's Gospel makes it clear that this passage does not refer to an event in which natural or supernatural forces will devastate a town, a region or the known world; rather, like so many of Jesus' warnings in Luke, it refers to the time when the enemy armies will invade and wreak sudden destruction. The warnings of Jesus came true in A.D. 70, but the promise of the kingdom remains. It may be that some time in the future ruin will break in on those who have not heeded God's call, but this is not what this passage is about.

The passage holds out an invitation, to this day, to those who are anxious about the future: God's sovereign rule of the world and his healing love are not only yours for the grasping but are waiting for your help.

OPEN

In what area of your life do you wish you exhibited more faith?

For Family

STUDY

1. *Read Luke 17:1-19.* The first two verses consider things people do to trip others up. Thinking back over the last two chapters, what might these things be referring to?

2. In what ways are the first three verses especially important for Christian leaders and teachers to hear and to heed?

3. Jesus' approach to forgiveness (17:3-4) is utterly different than basic human nature. How is forgiving someone like making yourself their servant rather than their master?

4. Perhaps not surprisingly, the disciples realize in verse 5 that all this will require more faith than they think they have. What does Jesus teach them about the nature of faith in verses 5-6?

5. How do verses 7-10 illustrate the proper perspective that we should have toward God? *He is our master*

6. Look at verse 10. How does this offer a common thread that ties together the short sayings of Jesus found in 17:1-10?

7. In verses 11-19, what parts of the story of the ten lepers are surprising?

8. How do gratitude and humility go hand in hand in the story of the lepers?

Jesus' closing words to the Samaritan invite a closer look. The word for "get up" or "rise" is a word early Christians would have recognized as having to do with resurrection. Like the prodigal son, this man was dead, and is alive again. New life, the life which Israel was longing for as part of the age to come, had arrived in his village that day, and it had called out of him a faith he didn't know he had.

9. *Read Luke 17:20-37.* There has been a growth industry in books and movies based on passages like this where one person is taken and the other left. Some have assumed the one taken is snatched up to heaven to be with God and the other is left to survive in a world devoid of believers. The passage actually works the other way around. The people who are taken are the ones in danger; they are being taken away by hostile forces. The word for "vultures" (v. 37) is the same word as "eagles"—which may well be a cryptic reference to the Roman legions, with the eagle as their imperial badge.

How does seeing this imagery as Jesus' symbolic and indirect description of what will happen when Rome comes in force make sense of the warnings (verses 20-37)?

10. The question from the Pharisees (17:20) implies that they think Jesus has a timetable in mind, in which certain things would happen in a particular order so that one could mark them off and get ready for the final drama. Part of Jesus' answer, as we have seen, is that it won't be like that. Life will go on as normal until the last moment.

No, God's kingdom isn't the sort of thing for which there are advance signs. Rather, he says, God's kingdom is within your grasp or in your midst (17:21). What does he mean then by this?

11. If the kingdom of God is in our midst, in our grasp, what implications does that have for us now?

PRAY

The rhythm of faith and gratitude seen in the stories in this chapter are simply what being a Christian is all about. There is an old spiritual discipline of listing one's blessings, naming them before God and giving thanks. It's a healthy thing to do, especially in a world where we too often assume we have an absolute right to health, happiness and every possible creature comfort. Spend this prayer time exercising this spiritual discipline.

HUMILITY AND TRUST

Luke 18

Picture yourself in a first-century courtroom. Here is the plaintiff, claiming eagerly that he has been wronged by the person opposing him. He has his team of lawyers, and they are arguing the case, producing witnesses, trying to persuade the judge that he is in the right. Here, opposite, is the defendant, the man the plaintiff is accusing. He and his team are trying to persuade the judge that *he* is in the right. In the ancient Jewish law court, all cases were like that, not just civil ones. If someone had stolen from you, you had to bring the charge yourself; you couldn't get the police to do it for you. If someone had murdered a relative, the same would be true.

So every legal case in Jesus' day was a matter of a judge deciding to vindicate one party or the other. The parables that Jesus begins this chapter with are both in some ways depicting a lawsuit.

OPEN

Describe a time where you had to plead your case with someone, where you had to try to convince someone that you were right.

STUDY

1. *Read Luke 18:1-14.* How are the two parables similar and different?

   Topic - similarly about prayer, dispects
   Different - audience - disciple, arrogant
   others =

2. Though some translations use the word *justify* or *justice* in verses 3, 5, 8 and 14, it could also be translated as "vindicate" or "vindication." What is meant by this in the context of each of the two parables?

3. How does the picture of the unjust judge in the first parable help us understand what God is actually like instead (vv. 1-8)?

   The stark contrast

   The first parable assumes that God's people are like litigants in a lawsuit, waiting for God's verdict. What is the lawsuit about? It seems to be about Israel, or rather now the renewed Israel gathered around Jesus, awaiting from God the vindication that will come when those who have opposed his message are finally routed. It is, in other words, about the same scenario as described in the previous chapter: the time when, through the final destruction of the city and temple that have opposed him, Jesus' followers will know that God has vindicated Jesus himself, and them as his followers. Though this moment will itself be terrifying, it will function as the liberating, vindicating judgment that God's people have been waiting and praying for. And if this is true of that final moment, it is also true of all such lesser moments, with which Christian living is filled.

4. How does the second parable, though describing a religious occasion, actually bear similarities to another lawsuit (vv. 9-14)?

    A plea to be found right

5. How is the conclusion of this parable, that the tax collector went home vindicated, such a great comfort?

    Hope for all

These two parables together make a powerful statement about what, in Paul's language, is called "justification by faith." The wider context is the final law court, in which God's chosen people will be vindicated after their life of suffering, holiness and service. Though enemies outside and inside may denounce and attack them, God will act and show that they truly are his people. But what Jesus is saying here—just as Paul says in Romans and Galatians—is that this future verdict is already known, in the present, when someone turns from sin and trusts God to be merciful.

6. *Read 18:15-30.* Contrast the little children in verses 15-17 with the rich ruler in verses 18-25. *trusting, no preconceptions*

7. How do children perfectly demonstrate the humble trust that Jesus has been speaking of?

8. What makes the rich ruler respond with sadness?

9. Jesus was putting into operation that for which most Jews had longed: God's kingdom, God's sovereign saving power operating in a new way for the benefit of the whole world. This meant that already, in the present, the period of time they spoke of as "the age to come" was breaking in. It would come fully in the future, when all evil had been done away with, and then those who belonged to it would share "the life of the coming age." Because the word for "age" here is often translated "eternal," the phrase "eternal life" has regularly been used to describe this life.

   In God's new age, everything would be new, fresh, and free from corruption, decay, evil, bitterness, pain, fear, and death. And this is what Jesus was bringing in the present. Where Jesus was, and where people with humble and penitent trust accepted that God's kingdom was active in and through him, there the life of the new age began to be seen.

   How can the church be a living example of this new age to come?

10. *Read 18:31-43.* Compare and contrast the disciples in verses 31-34 with the blind man in verses 35-43.

11. Once again (in v. 42) Jesus tells someone that their faith has been the means of their rescue. How does this episode show that faith is not just an inner feeling but also outward action?

12. In Luke's story, we have almost arrived in Jerusalem. On the one hand, this is the place where the forces of darkness are gathering, and will wreak their worst fury on Jesus himself. Behind that is the warning on the city and the temple if they do not accept Jesus' offer of peace. On the other hand, the powers of the new age are already at work: healing, welcome, joy and excitement. There is still so much we do not understand in the world, but Jesus has already taken the full weight of evil on himself. So the things we still need to face hold no terrors for us. Equally, there is so much already given to us when we humbly believe and trust in God's power.

In what ways do you find yourself fearing the unknown and the difficult things that you are facing, and also humbly trusting Jesus' power in your life?

PRAY

Sit in silence and allow God to speak to you. He may wish to point out places in your life which need the power of the Spirit which is accessible to you through Christ's resurrection, or he may gently point out the places which do not reflect humility and faith.

THE TRIUMPHAL ENTRY

Luke 19

Mile after mile, you wind up through the sandy hills from Jericho, the lowest point on the face of the earth, through the Judean desert, climbing all the way. Halfway up, you reach sea level; you've already climbed a long way from the Jordan valley, and you still have to ascend a fair-sized mountain. The sense of relief and excitement when you reach the summit is intense. At last you exchange barren, dusty desert for lush green growth. At last you stop climbing, you crest the summit, and there before you, glistening in the sun, is the holy city, Jerusalem itself. The end of the journey; the pilgrimage to end all pilgrimages; Passover time in the city of God.

That was the way the pilgrims came, with Jesus going on ahead, as he had planned all along. This was to be the climax of his story, of his public career, of his vocation. He knew well enough what lay ahead, and had set his face to go and meet it head on. He couldn't stop announcing the kingdom, but that announcement could only come true if he now embodied in himself the things he'd been talking about. This was to be the moment of God's new exodus, God's great Passover, and nothing could stop Jesus going ahead to celebrate it.

OPEN

Identify an area of your life where Jesus might be asking you to follow him into a difficult place, to do something scary or to face struggle.

STUDY

1. *Read Luke 19:1-10.* Why would everyone in Jericho have disliked Zacchaeus?

2. Here Jesus doesn't tell a parable as he has been doing, like that of the prodigal son. Rather the tax collector himself speaks to Jesus in public. In what ways does Zacchaeus give evidence of his extravagant repentance in this story?

3. How is the story of Zacchaeus a kind of balance to the previous story of the rich ruler?

4. How do these stories speak to how we should view and deal with our possessions and money?

5. *Read Luke 19:11-27.* This parable has echoes of the story of Archelaus, the older brother of Herod Antipas, a story Jesus' hearers would have

been familiar with. After the death of their father, Herod the Great, in 4 B.C., Archelaus went to Rome to be confirmed as king, followed by a delegation of Judeans who didn't want him. (Ten years later, after much misrule, he went again, only to find another delegation of Jews and Samaritans opposing his appointment—this time successfully.) But Jesus has several new twists and meanings to the story.

For most of church history this parable has been taken as a picture of the last judgment. In this light, who do the king, the servants and the subjects who hated the nobleman in this parable represent?

6. But the parable also has something to say about events much closer to Jesus' own day.

    How is this parable a description of what Jesus himself is doing by coming to Jerusalem?

7. What does this parable say to us today as we await the final day of God's judgment, the final "coming" of Jesus to our world?

8. *Read Luke 19:28-48.* What are all the different indications in verses 28-40 that this event is a royal occasion for Jesus?

9. Jesus comes himself as the fulfillment of the nation's hopes, answering their longings for a king who would bring peace to earth from

heaven itself. Yet there are still grumblers. Why are the Pharisees anxious about this occasion?

10. What brings Jesus to tears as he views Jerusalem in verses 41-44?

11. How do Jesus' tears in verses 41-44 go together with his actions in the temple in verses 45-48?

12. The crowds cheer for Jesus and sing his praises, but if they had understood his own Passover action on the cross that was coming, they would have been puzzled and distressed, as indeed they soon will be.

Are we only willing to follow Jesus when he does what we want, or are we willing to follow him into trouble, controversy, trial and death? What does it mean for us today to follow in times of such difficulty?

PRAY

Think about your answer to the introductory question. Pray for the strength not only to praise Jesus but also to truly follow him wherever he calls you. Jesus' triumphal entry was indeed a royal occasion worthy of praise and adoration. Yet he would soon face the cross, and his disciples would have to choose to follow him or not.

Debates with Jesus

Luke 20:1–21:4

Many churches possess a sequence of pictures that, together, tell a complete story. Sometimes these are in the windows or painted on the walls or the ceiling. What look like distinct pictures, when you "read" them one after the other, in fact tell a complete story.

The debates in Luke 20 are just like that. They tell, in miniature, the whole story of Jesus. They are a summary of the gospel. Jesus emerges from John's prophetic movement; he is anointed as Messiah. He comes to Israel, to the towns of Galilee, and ultimately to Jerusalem, with a message of warning and pleading. He is rejected and handed over to Caesar's men for execution and on the third day he is raised from the dead. As a result, his followers discover that he is the Messiah. The sequence of these debates can hardly be accidental.

OPEN

Often protestors will perform symbolic actions that represent what they actually want to say, such as burning a flag (itself a symbol) or temporarily blockading a road. Why are such symbolic actions often powerful ways of getting a point across?

STUDY

1. *Read Luke 20:1-26.* Looking back to the end of Luke 19 we see Jesus throwing out those who were selling things in the temple. The question the Jewish leaders ask in Luke 20:1-8 about where he got his authority to command what does and doesn't go on in the Temple is a natural one to ask.

   Jesus' answer takes them by surprise and does not seem natural at all. What are the connections Jesus is trying to make here between himself and John the Baptist?

2. We have the task of making Christ's lordship known. Normally it wouldn't be appropriate to overturn tables and expel people from buildings. What symbolic actions might be appropriate in our world, to make the point that Jesus possesses all authority in heaven and on earth?

3. No self-respecting first-century monarch would ever have allowed himself to get in the position described in 20:9-19, and no landowner would tolerate for very long that kind of behavior. But there are striking parallels between this story and the last parable that Jesus told (19:11-27).

   How does this parable of the tenants also explain what was happening in Jesus' coming to Jerusalem?

4. In Luke 20:17, Jesus quotes from Psalm 118:22 (the same psalm echoed by the crowds in 19:38; it was, after all, a psalm of pilgrimage). How does this make the point of Jesus' story absolutely clear?

5. The coins the Romans made the Jews use to pay taxes flouted Jewish law by using a picture of a human being (Caesar himself, of course) and by describing him in words that a Jew would regard as blasphemous, describing Caesar as the son of a god.

   What made the question that was posed to Jesus by the spies in Luke 20:20-26 a trick question?

6. The audience now supposes that Jesus is on the spot, about to be found out, when suddenly everything is reversed. How does Jesus turn the accusers into the accused and challenge the authorities in the temple?

7. What does it mean today to give back to God what belongs to him?

8. *Read Luke 20:27–21:4.* Now the Sadducees have a question for Jesus. They were the aristocracy of Judaism, including most of the leading priestly families, who relied only on the first five books of the Old Testament. They therefore denied the resurrection of the dead, presumably because they did not see justification for it in

Genesis through Deuteronomy. The Pharisees, however, believed
in the resurrection.

When Jews thought of "the resurrection," they looked into the future when God would raise all Israel, perhaps even all humans, from
the dead, and create a new world for them to live in. This hope was
not about what we think of as "life after death," a non-bodily state in
which people simply went on existing in some form or other. It was
about a future event that had not yet happened, as a result of which
the dead would be alive again in a way they weren't at present, and
all the wrongs of the world would be put right.

What points does Jesus makes in response to the question from the
Sadducees in verses 27-40?

9. Jesus now has his own riddle to ask. He quotes Psalm 110, a psalm
    of David about the Messiah who will be enthroned until victory is
    attained over those who have opposed him, and who will be exalted,
    bringing judgment on the unjust.

    How does Jesus expand the understanding of "Messiah" for his audi-
    ence through his use of Psalm 110 in 20:41-44?

10. The stone will be rejected but they will find that Jesus will be vin-
    dicated. He will be seen as the true Messiah. He will build the true
    temple, and will himself be the standard by which everything and
    everyone else will be judged. God's way of measuring reality is not
    our way. The box labeled "messiahship" is bigger than anyone had
    realized. So the stone will be rejected, but they will find that Jesus
    will be vindicated. He will be seen as the true Messiah. He will build

the true temple, and will himself be the standard by which everything and everyone else will be judged.

What agendas and ways of thinking do you have, and how might they be too small in the light of God's reality?

11. How does Jesus then contrast the teachers of the law and the widow in 20:45–21:4?

12. To what specific persons or situations can you as a follower of Jesus today take these larger realities and values of the Messiah?

PRAY

Pray in response to the things in this study that stirred your heart. After a few minutes pray about the truths that God highlighted for you.

NOTE ON LUKE 20:36

Jesus doesn't say that those who are raised will become angels but that they will be like or equal to angels. That is, those who are raised will live in a deathless, immortal state. Neither is Jesus suggesting that the resurrection will not be bodily, merely that the bodies of the raised will be, in significant ways, quite unlike our present ones. Those whom God counts worthy of "the age to come," as opposed to "the present age" (Luke 20:34-35), will have bodies appropriate for the new world in which death will be no more.

WATCHING FOR
THE SON OF MAN

Luke 21:5-38

NKJV

In Jesus' day dramatic and unexpected happenings in the night sky were often thought to signify more than just physical disaster as large objects crashed to earth. People looked at them carefully because they believed they would tell them about the imminent rise and fall of kings and empires. And when Jesus' disciples asked him how they would know when the frightening events he was talking about would take place, that's probably the sort of thing they had in mind. Surely Jesus would want them to know, and so would give them signs to watch out for?

Jesus will give them signs of a sort, but actually the main thing he wants them to learn is that there will be a period of waiting, when they will have to be patient through dangerous and testing times.

OPEN

In what kinds of situations do you have the hardest time waiting for something?

STUDY

1. *Read Luke 21:5-38.* The temple, the most beautiful building imaginable to the Jews, adorned and decorated by the skill and love of hundreds of craftsmen over many decades, and occupying the central place in national life and religion—Jesus said this temple would be torn down. This was unthinkable for devout Jews.

   What does Jesus say to watch for on a worldwide level (vv. 8-11)?

   Wars & natural catastrophes, famines, disease, signs from heaven

2. Jesus warns in verse 8 about deceptions in which people will use Jesus' name or announce that the time has come. What could those deceptions look like today? *Prosperity gospel, crystals & spirituality*

3. According to verses 12-19, what will life be like for those who claim to be followers of Christ during the time Jesus is referring to?

   the persecution → gain life

4. What promises does Jesus offer to his followers (in verses 12-19) regarding this time of waiting and turmoil?

   the Spirit will provide words & wisdom

5. How do these provide the comfort and encouragement needed in times of suffering and persecution for believers in Jesus' time and for us today?

6. Verses 20-24 fit with everything Luke has reported Jesus as saying up to this point. A time of crisis is coming, in which the failure of Israel in general and Jerusalem in particular to repent and follow the kingdom-way advocated by Jesus would have its disastrous result.

   Jesus doesn't name in verse 20 the foreign power whose armies will surround Jerusalem. His listeners would have assumed he was talking about Rome, and later readers would recognize the fall of the temple in A.D. 70 at the hands of Roman forces as the fulfillment of Jesus' prophecies here.

   In verses 20-24, what instructions does Jesus give to his followers for when this event occurs?

7. Why does Jesus suggest that they had no duty to stay in Jerusalem, that it was not worth defending?

8. "Signs in the sun, the moon and the stars" (v. 25) could mean just that. But such a phrase was well known in Luke's day as a regular code for talking about the great nations and kingdoms of the earth and how they would be, as we say in our own picture language, "going through convulsions." Certainly, the rest of verse 25 and verse 26 suggest as much.

   The coming of the Son of Man must then be understood, as first-century Jews would certainly have understood it, as the fulfillment of the prophecy of Daniel 7. One of the most popular prophecies of the day, this passage is best understood as a promise that, when the Jerusalem that had opposed Jesus' message was overthrown, this would be the vindication of Jesus and his people, the sign that he had been enthroned at his Father's side in heaven (see Luke 20:42-43).

While the destruction of the temple is long in the past, what do verses 20-33 tell us about living in a world which, like Jerusalem, often refuses Jesus' message?

9. In verses 34-36, how does Jesus say his followers are to live while they wait for the great crisis, the destruction of Jerusalem?

10. Followers of Jesus today are also in a waiting time. In our day-to-day lives, what can make following Jesus a wearying and difficult path?

11. How do verses 34-36 speak to us today as followers of Jesus?

12. There are times when our eyes will be shutting with tiredness, spiritual, mental, emotional and physical. The life of faith, at times, is not an exciting battle with adrenaline flowing and banners flying but the steady tread of prayer, hope, Scripture, sacrament and witness, day by day and week by week.

    What can we, as followers of Christ today, do to help each other live by patience in these times?

PRAY

In prayer, honestly put before Jesus the struggle, weariness or fatigue that you are feeling. Pray for the fruits of the Spirit, particularly patience.

NOTE ON LUKE 21:27

The phrase "the coming of the Son of Man" has been much misunderstood in the scholarly world as well as in the popular sense of a human figure traveling downward toward the earth on actual clouds. The word *coming* in Greek could mean either "coming" or "going." Even if we agree that "coming" is to be the preferred translation, that would still not mean that the author intends us to understand the movement of the Son of Man to be downward from heaven to earth. The reason is that Daniel 7 (from which this passage derives) conceives the scene from the perspective of heaven, not earth. The Son of Man figure "comes" to the Ancient of Days, *from* earth *to* heaven, vindicated after suffering. (See N. T. Wright, *Jesus and the Victory of God,* p. 361.)

Luke certainly believes in the "second coming" of Jesus, as Acts 1:11 indicates. It's just that this is not what he (or Jesus) has in mind in Luke 21 since the movement is toward heaven not earth. Rather, as said above, this enthronement is the vindication of Jesus, who said that Jerusalem and the temple were under judgment for wandering so far away from God's original calling.

CELEBRATION
AND BETRAYAL

Luke 22

Imagine a manager or coach trying to prepare a team for the match of their lives. They are facing their greatest opponents. The coach needs them to be totally focused on the task in hand. He has just outlined the strategy they must follow and warns them about the team they will face. He has explained to them that they have come a long way, and he has warned the captain that he will have a tough game, but it will be all right in the end. He has told them that he won't be with them on the field so they will have to think for themselves.

Unfortunately, the team then squabbles about who is the best player, the captain ignores the coach's warning about his performance, and the coach, frustrated by the team's response, ends the speech and moves on.

This is a superficial example of the events that take place in chapter 22 of Luke's Gospel as Jesus tries to prepare his disciples for the things they are about to experience in the hours ahead.

OPEN

Describe a time when you were part of a group (maybe the leader) that wasn't cooperating with the leader or following instructions well. What were the causes of the trouble?

STUDY

1. *Read Luke 22:1-38.* In what ways is the event in verses 1-23 a story of both celebration and betrayal?

2. Many helpful theories have been proposed over the centuries about how it was that Jesus dealt with our sins. At this point, however, Jesus did not give his followers a theory but an act to perform.

    This meal was, first and foremost, a Passover meal (Luke 22:1). Hundreds of years before, when the powers of evil that were enslaving God's people were at their worst, God acted through Moses and Aaron to judge Egypt and save Israel. And the sign and means of both judgment and rescue was the Passover: the angel of death struck down the firstborn of all Egypt, but spared Israel as the firstborn of God, "passing over" their houses because of the blood of the lamb on the doorposts (Exodus 12).

    What does this tell us about the meaning of the meal Jesus ate with his disciples and of Jesus' death?
    The blood of Jesus identifies us to be spa[...]
    We are spared

3. How does Jesus' idea of greatness contrast with that of the world in verses 24-30?

Those who serve loyally

4. How does Jesus show his care for others in Luke 22:31-32, even as he was facing the most intense trial of his life?

Praying for the disciples

5. In Luke 22:36 Jesus quotes from the last verse of the great Servant Song of Isaiah 52:13–53:12. Jesus was fulfilling, and knew he was fulfilling, the scriptural prophesies about this figure who suffered injustice for others and was abandoned and seemingly defeated, exactly as the Scripture had foretold.

   How do we see the sheer aloneness of Jesus throughout the Last Supper?

6. *Read 22:39-71.* Why is it so important that the disciples pray (verse 46)?

Avoid temptation

7. Like many Jews of his day, Jesus believed that Israel's history, and with it world history, would pass into a moment of great terror and darkness, and that God's redemption, the coming kingdom, would emerge the other side. This would be the "trial," the "test," the "great tribulation." Unlike other leaders of the day, Jesus believed that it was his appointed task to go into that darkness, that terror, all by himself, to carry the fate of Israel and the world through to the other side.

Jesus has known that this is his role, and in fact has just foretold his death to the disciples at the Last Supper. What makes him now shrink from the role in the garden (verses 39-46)?

8. How does Luke highlight Jesus' faith and truth as he tells what happened the night Jesus was arrested in verses 54-71?

9. Think of the fireside, that chilly April night. Loyalty has taken Peter this far, but as the night wears on tiredness has sapped his resolve. It's a familiar problem, which strikes often, for us, in the middle of life or of some great project. We begin with excitement but our intentions or energy drain away.

   In what ways do you relate to Peter's attempts and struggles to be faithful?

10. What are the similarities and differences with Peter and Judas?

11. What injustices does Jesus suffer as described in verses 54-71?

12. Peter's weakness, the guards' bullying, the court's perversion of justice—all this and much more put Jesus on the cross. It wasn't just a theological transaction; it was real sin, real human folly and

rebellion, the dehumanized humanity that has lost its way and spat in God's face. Have we not, in our own way, done so as well? Where do you see yourself in this story?

PRAY

Spend time in confession. Jesus entered the darkness and the horror to bring redemption for all of us and rescue us from our sin. Lay before him the places where you have acted in rebellion, unbelief and sin like the characters in this chapter.

NOTE ON LUKE 22:36-38

Jesus had won an initial victory of the forces of evil at an earlier stage. Now, however, he faces the greatest battle of all, which will involve him being hunted down as though he were a lawless brigand.

If Jesus himself is to go unprotected in the face of the last enemy, his followers need to watch out for themselves. They don't understand, however, that he's talking in pictures, and seem to think he means them to get ready for an actual fight. When Jesus says "That's enough!" he isn't suggesting that two swords would be sufficient for the job in hand (what could that possibly mean?); he is wearily putting a stop to the entire conversation, in which at every point the disciples seem determined to misunderstand him.

25

THE CRUCIFIXION

Luke 23

Herod has been in the background throughout the Gospel. Luke tells us that he had wanted to hunt Jesus down and kill him much earlier, during Jesus' Galilean ministry (13:31); Luke now gives us this scene where they meet at last, the present and precarious "king of the Jews" face to face with the real and coming King. Herod saw Jesus as a combination of John the Baptist, who had fascinated him with his talk but frightened him with his warnings, and the kind of circus artist who can do magic tricks to order.

Jesus disappoints him. He says nothing and does no miracles. We might have expected that, like Moses at the court of Pharaoh, the leader of the new exodus would either threaten Herod with God's judgment or perform remarkable feats to demonstrate his claims, but Jesus does neither. Luke, for whom Jesus is certainly both a true prophet and the true king of the Jews, places this meeting in a sequence of scenes designed to reveal the truth of this kingship and the falsehood of all other types. At this moment, the truth is more eloquently stated by silence.

OPEN

Think of a time you or someone you know was falsely accused. What's the natural reaction of the accused in such cases, and why?

Shock & anger

STUDY

1. *Read Luke 23:1-26.* What case do the Pharisees and other Jewish leaders make against Jesus?

   Stirring up people, Opposing tax payment claiming to be a "King"

2. Why are Pilate and Herod hesitant to condemn Jesus when they should be quite interested in doing away with rebel leaders?

   Numerous followers, Pilate finds no cause

3. Among the Evangelists, Luke has the most interesting cast of minor characters, two of whom come into focus in this section. How are we to see ourselves in the figure of Barabbas?

   undeserving, but set free as

4. Simon of Cyrene had come on pilgrimage to Jerusalem from one of the Jewish communities in North Africa, and found himself a pilgrim in a very different sense. Describe the ways that Simon is a model for followers of Christ.

5. Though Barabbas and Simon are the key to this passage, how should we identify with the crowds in the story as well?

   Crowd mentality = following the group

6. *Read 23:27-56.* What interchange does Jesus have with the women in
    verses 27-31?

Jesus knows he is unjustly dying the death of a brigand, a holy revolutionary. If Israel refuses to follow him and repent of violent rebellion
against Rome, he knows the fate in store for the nation will make his
crucifixion seem mild by comparison. That, of course, is what happens in A.D. 70 when Rome brutally crushes Israel's revolt. So, he tells
the women, if they do this to the green wood, it will be even worse for
the dry wood. In other words, if they do this to the prince of peace,
we can only imagine what they will do to genuine warlords.

7. Luke 23:32-43 is full of contrasts. Which ones stand out to you?

8. How does Luke fill the story of the death of Jesus in verses 44-56
    with eyewitnesses?

9. What details about the death and burial of Jesus does Luke include
    to prove Jesus' innocence and that he actually died?

10. In what ways does the story in verses 44-56 already give signs of what is to come?

torn veil, delay for Sabbath
Jesus trusting God with His spirit

11. With which character in chapter 23 (Pilate, Herod, the Pharisees and other Jewish leaders, Barabbas, Simon, the crowds, the women, the two thieves, the centurion, Joseph) evokes the strongest response in you, and why?

12. Luke began his book by telling Theophilus that he could rely on these facts, and in chapter 23 he presents his witnesses one by one. But it is not just the facts of Jesus' death and burial that Luke is interested in. He is equally clear that Jesus dies an innocent, righteous man, and that he is bearing in himself the fate he had predicted so often for the warlike nation. The One was bearing the sins of the many.

What aspect of the story of Jesus' trial, death and burial has moved you in studying this chapter, and why?

PRAY

Take a few moments to pause in prayer, reflection and worship.

NOTE ON LUKE 23:50-56

Jewish burial customs varied considerably, but in this case the burial was to be in two stages. First, the body would be laid on a ledge in a cave, in this case a man-made one (though many natural caves were used for the same purpose). It would be wrapped up, with spices and ointments to cover the smell of rotting flesh. The expense this would incur was necessary because the tomb would be used again, perhaps several times, in the coming months before decay was complete; other bodies would be place on other ledges.

When all the flesh had rotted away, in the second stage the remaining bones would be reverently collected and placed in a small ossuary, a bone-box. Unlike modern Western burials, therefore (and of course quite unlike cremations), an initial burial of this sort marked a stage on the road of saying a farewell, not the end of that road. Luke doesn't tell us, but he assumes we know, that tombs like this were shut with a large rolling stone across the door (see 24:2).

This is why it is important to know which tomb it was, and that it was a tomb which had never been used before. There was no chance of a mistake, as there might have been had there been three or four bodies, at different stages of decomposition, on various shelves in a dark cave.

THE RESURRECTION

Luke 24

Jesus had spoken of his own resurrection at various stages, from Luke 9:22 onward. Two of his greatest stories had ended with a strong reference to rising from the dead (15:24, 32; 16:31). But nobody had truly heard what he was saying. They were puzzled, and understandably so; "resurrection," in that world, was what God would do in the end for all the righteous dead, giving new embodiment to everyone from Abraham, Isaac and Jacob down to the most recent righteous martyrs.

Though people could speak of a prophet like Elijah or John the Baptist returning from the dead, what they probably meant by that was that someone would come who seemed to embody the same spirit. "The resurrection" itself would be a large-scale event. After Israel's great and final suffering, all God's people would be given new life, new bodies.

We shouldn't be surprised, then, at how surprised they were on the first Easter morning.

OPEN

When were you surprised—even stunned—by something?

STUDY

1. *Read Luke 24:1-12.* What was the opening mood of the women and apostles on Easter morning?

2. Luke reports that women were the first to find the empty tomb and that the apostles didn't believe the report was true. (Women were not regarded as reliable witnesses in the ancient world.) If Luke were making this story up a generation or more after the event, as some suggest, how might he have written the story instead?

3. *Read 24:13-35.* Why was the crucifixion so devastating for the followers of Jesus?

4. The couple on the road to Emmaus may well have been husband and wife, Cleopas and Mary (see John 19:25; "Clopas" there is probably the same person as "Cleopas" here).

   What kept Cleopas and his companion from recognizing Jesus?

5. How can this story of Jesus' encounter with the pair offer a model for us as we find ourselves in difficulties, confusion or grief?

6. Jesus explained to the confused pair what *had* to happen to the Messiah from the whole Old Testament, beginning with the five books of Moses. Just as God redeemed Israel from slavery in Egypt at the first Passover, now at this last Passover Israel was redeemed by God. Liberated from pagan domination, sin, the power of the evil one and death itself, the new Israel was set free in a new exodus to serve God in peace and holiness. He now invites his followers on a journey to a new promised land.

   The two on the road had been seeing the history of Israel as the story of how God would redeem Israel *from* suffering, but it was instead the story of how God would redeem Israel *through* suffering. Perhaps Luke is saying that we can only know Jesus, can only recognize him, when we learn to see him within the true story of God, Israel and the world.

   How can we grow in our ability to see Jesus this way?

7. What are the similarities and differences between the meal in verses 28-35 and the very first meal recorded in the Bible in Genesis 3:6-7?

   eyes opened - seeing/recognizing sin vs God's salvation.

8. Luke intended that his readers should see the simple meal here pointing forward to the breaking of bread, which quickly became the central symbolic action of Jesus' people. Jesus was recognized by the couple in the breaking of the bread (v. 35). How is he also made known to us in the Lord's Supper or Communion?

The story of the couple on the road to Emmaus frames the entire Gospel with the story of another couple at its beginning in 2:41-52. There, after three days, Mary and Joseph also find the Jesus they thought they had lost and are also greeted by his strange words about what *had* to happen, that it was necessary to do his Father's work.

9. *Read 24:36-53.* Based on these verses, what sort of body do you think Jesus had after he was raised from the dead?

10. What are the elements of the mission of the church as seen in 24:36-53?

11. What kinds of changes, for individuals and for nations, can repentance and forgiveness lead to (24:47)?

12. How are you and your faith community participating in this mission?

PRAY

Luke's Gospel ends, as it began, in the temple at Jerusalem. Worship of the living God, now revealed in Jesus of Nazareth, is at the heart of Luke's vision of the Christian life. Worship him now.

GUIDELINES FOR LEADERS

My grace is sufficient for you.
(2 Corinthians 12:9)

If leading a small group is something new for you, don't worry. These sessions are designed to flow naturally and be led easily. You may even find that the studies seem to lead themselves!

This study guide is flexible. You can use it with a variety of groups—students, professionals, coworkers, friends, neighborhood or church groups. Each study takes forty-five to sixty minutes in a group setting.

You don't need to be an expert on the Bible or a trained teacher to lead a small group. These guides are designed to facilitate a group's discussion, not a leader's presentation. Guiding group members to discover together what the Bible has to say and to listen together for God's guidance will help them remember much more than a lecture would.

There are some important facts to know about group dynamics and encouraging discussion. The suggestions listed below should equip you to effectively and enjoyably fulfill your role as leader.

PREPARING FOR THE STUDY

1. Ask God to help you understand and apply the passage in your own life. Unless this happens, you will not be prepared to lead others. Pray too for the various members of the group. Ask God to open

your hearts to the message of his Word and motivate you to action.

2. Read the introduction to the entire guide to get an overview of the topics that will be explored.

3. As you begin each study, read and reread the assigned Bible passage to familiarize yourself with it. This study guide is based on the For Everyone series on the New Testament (published by SPCK and Westminster John Knox). It will help you and the group if you have on hand a copy of the companion volume from the For Everyone series both for the translation of the passage found there and for further insight into the passage.

4. Carefully work through each question in the study. Spend time in meditation and reflection as you consider how to respond.

5. Write your thoughts and responses in the space provided in the study guide. This will help you to express your understanding of the passage clearly.

6. It may help to have a Bible dictionary handy. Use it to look up any unfamiliar words, names or places. The glossary at the end of each New Testament for Everyone commentary may likewise be helpful for keeping discussion moving.

7. Reflect seriously on how you need to apply the Scripture to your life. Remember that the group members will follow your lead in responding to the studies. They will not go any deeper than you do.

LEADING THE STUDY

1. At the beginning of your first time together, explain that these studies are meant to be discussions, not lectures. Encourage the members of the group to participate. However, do not put pressure on those who may be hesitant to speak—especially during the first few sessions.

2. Be sure that everyone in your group has a study guide. Encourage the group to prepare beforehand for each discussion by reading the introduction to the guide and by working through the questions in each study.

3. Begin each study on time. Open with prayer, asking God to help the group to understand and apply the passage.

4. Have a group member read aloud the introduction at the beginning of the discussion.

5. Discuss the "Open" question before the Bible passage is read. The "Open" question introduces the theme of the study and helps group members to begin to open up, and can reveal where our thoughts and feelings need to be transformed by Scripture. Reading the passage first will tend to color the honest reactions people would otherwise give—because they are, of course, supposed to think the way the Bible does. Encourage as many members as possible to respond to the "Open" question, and be ready to get the discussion going with your own response.

6. Have a group member read aloud the passage to be studied as indicated in the guide.

7. The study questions are designed to be read aloud just as they are written. You may, however, prefer to express them in your own words.

   There may be times when it is appropriate to deviate from the study guide. For example, a question may have already been answered. If so, move on to the next question. Or someone may raise an important question not covered in the guide. Take time to discuss it, but try to keep the group from going off on tangents.

8. Avoid answering your own questions. An eager group quickly becomes passive and silent if members think the leader will do most of the talking. If necessary repeat or rephrase the question until it is clearly understood, or refer to the commentary woven into the guide to clarify the context or meaning.

9. Don't be afraid of silence in response to the discussion questions. People may need time to think about the question before formulating their answers.

10. Don't be content with just one answer. Ask, "What do the rest of you think?" or "Anything else?" until several people have given answers to the question.

11. Try to be affirming whenever possible. Affirm participation. Never reject an answer; if it is clearly off-base, ask, "Which verse led you to that conclusion?" or again, "What do the rest of you think?"

12. Don't expect every answer to be addressed to you, even though this will probably happen at first. As group members become more at ease, they will begin to truly interact with each other. This is one sign of healthy discussion.

13. Don't be afraid of controversy. It can be very stimulating. If you don't resolve an issue completely, don't be frustrated. Explain that the group will move on and God may enlighten all of you in later sessions.

14. Periodically summarize what the group has said about the passage. This helps to draw together the various ideas mentioned and gives continuity to the study. But don't preach.

15. Conclude your time together with the prayer suggestion at the end of the study, adapting it to your group's particular needs as appropriate. Ask for God's help in following through on the applications you've identified.

16. End on time.

Many more suggestions and helps for studying a passage or guiding discussion can be found in *How to Lead a LifeGuide Bible Study* and *The Big Book on Small Groups* (both from InterVarsity Press/USA).

Other InterVarsity Press Resources from N. T. Wright

The Challenge of Jesus
N. T. Wright offers clarity and a full accounting of the facts of the life and teachings of Jesus, revealing how the Son of God was also solidly planted in first-century Palestine. *978-0-8308-2200-3, 202 pages, hardcover*

The Challenge of Easter
The meaning of Easter seems lost among the colored eggs and chocolate candies. In this excerpt from *The Challenge of Jesus,* Wright explains Easter's bold, almost unbelievable claim: Jesus has risen from the dead. Here is God's announcement of an invitation to live as though God is among us, making everything new.

Resurrection
This 50-minute DVD confronts the most startling claim of Christianity—that Jesus rose from the dead. Shot on location in Israel, Greece and England, N. T. Wright presents the political, historical and theological issues of Jesus' day and today regarding this claim. Wright brings clarity and insight to one of the most profound mysteries in human history. Study guide included. *978-0-8308-3435-8, DVD*

Evil and the Justice of God
N. T. Wright explores all aspects of evil and how it presents itself in society today. Fully grounded in the story of the Old and New Testaments, this presentation is provocative and hopeful; a fascinating analysis of and response to the fundamental question of evil and justice that faces believers. *978-0-8308-3398-6, 176 pages, hardcover*

Evil
Filmed in Israel, South Africa and England, this 50-minute DVD confronts some of the major "evil" issues of our time—from tsunamis to AIDS—and puts them under the biblical spotlight. N. T. Wright says there is a solution to the problem of evil, if only we have the honesty and courage to name it and understand it for what it is. Study guide included. *978-0-8308-3434-1, DVD*

Small Faith—Great God
N. T. Wright reminds us that what matters is not how much faith we have as Who our faith is in. Wright looks at the character of the faith God calls us to. He unfolds how dependence, humility and mystery all have a role to play. But the author doesn't ignore the messiness and difficulties of life, when hard times come and the unexpected knocks us down. He opens to us what faith means in times of trial and even in the face of death. Through it all he reminds us, it's

not great faith we need: it is faith in a great God. *978-0-8308-3833-2, 176 pages, hardcover*

Justification: God's Plan and Paul's Vision
In this comprehensive account and defense of the crucial doctrine of justification, Wright also responds to critics who have challenged what has come to be called the New Perspective. Ultimately, he provides a chance for those in the middle of and on both sides of the debate to interact directly with his views and form their own conclusions. *978-0-8308-3863-9, 279 pages, hardcover*

Colossians and Philemon
In Colossians, Paul presents Christ as "the firstborn over all creation," and appeals to his readers to seek a maturity found only Christ. In Philemon, Paul appeals to a fellow believer to receive a runaway slave in love and forgiveness. In this volume N. T. Wright offers comment on both of these important books. *978-0-8308-4242-1, 199 pages, paperback*